5 SNEAKING OUT. *Lynda Barry (chicago)* draws the weekly *Ernie Pook's Comeek*, collected in 5 books. Her first novel is *The Good Times Are Killing Me*.

13 THE BASKET CASE. *Jacques Tardi (paris)* has illustrated an edition of Celine's *Journey to the End of the Night* (Gallimard), which is a best seller in France.

37 THIS LITTLE PIGGY WENT TO MARKET. *Sue Coe (nyc)* has been working on her *Porkopolis* series for 3 years. *Andrew Tyler (london)* is a journalist for various papers.

55 MIDSUMMER DAY DREAMS. *Winsor McCay (1867-1934)* was one of the first and most influential comic strip artists. His *Little Nemo* is reprinted by Fantagraphics.

56 COLLECT YOURSELF. *Jerry Moriarty (nyc)* recently painted a subway poster for the School of Visual Arts. His previous "Crimes" appeared in *Picture Story*.

58 HE HAD A FUNNY FACE. *Drew Friedman (nyc)* is the coauthor, with brother Josh, of *Any Similarity to Persons Living or Dead* and the forthcoming *Warts and All*.

59 THE ROAD TO RANA POONA. *Kim Deitch (virginia)* draws the serial *A Shroud for Waldo. Beyond the Pale* (Fantagraphics) is a collection of his commix.

68 SWEET. *Joost Swarte (netherlands)* designed the '89 monthly for the avant garde theatre De Toneelschuur. His portfolio *RRRRRRR* features 7 drawings of cats.

72 THE SEVEN SEAS OF SIN. *David Sandlin (nyc)* shows paintings regularly at Gracie Mansion Gallery. His most recent book is *Land of 1,000 Beers* (SVA).

78 WAKING UP BLIND. *Chris Ware (austin)* currently attends the University of Texas. He has done strips for *The Daily Texan* regularly for the past 3 years.

82 COWBOY HENK. *Kamagurka and Herr Seele (Belgium)* collaborate on cartoons for various European magazines and comedy performances for Belgian TV.

83 OBA'S ELECTROPLATE FACTORY. *Yoshiharu Tsuge (japan)* worked in a rural electroplate factory in 1950. He later became an important contributor to *Garo*.

107 THE ULTIMATE DEBT. *Justin Green (california)* is compiling a book, *20 Years of the Ray-Boy's Adventures*. His work appears regularly in *Signs of the Times*.

109 OUTSIDE OUT. *Mark Beyer (in transit)* continues his weekly strip, *Amy and Jordan*, and draws a monthly feature for Japan's *Ryuko Tsushin Om*.

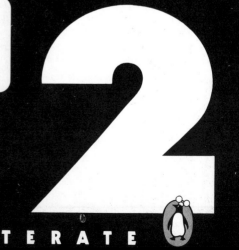

Design: Dale Crain

W 2

THE POST-LITERATE

CONTENTS, CONTINUED

115 BABE, DARLING OF THE HILLS. *Boody Rogers (texas)* is best known for *Sparky Watts,* the bizarre superhero who ran from the late 30's to early 50's.

131 FROM MARACAIBO. *Altan (italy),* the author of many children's books, contributes to the weeklies *Panorama* and *L'Unita,* as well as to the monthly *Linus.*

137 MAUS, CH. 9, AND HERE MY TROUBLES BEGAN. *art spiegelman (nyc)* estimates that completing his book will take 2 more years. He's been saying that for 11 years.

163 THE CHILD SLAVE REBELLION. *Henry Darger (1892-1973)* has had many posthumous gallery exhibits. He will be featured in the upcoming book *American Mysteries.*

175 I FELL ASLEEP WAITING FOR HER. *Jayr Pulga (new york),* an occasional contributor to *RAW,* is currently devoting most of his time to abstract painting.

178 GOOD OL' GREGOR BROWN. *R. Sikoryak (nyc),* the associate editor of *RAW,* is also the host of a weekly performance cabaret at the Pyramid Club.

180 THE CORNER LOCATION. *Ben Katchor (nyc),* recipient of the 1990 Swann Foundation Award, draws the weekly *Julius Knipl, Real Estate Photographer.*

186 REALITY. *Marti (barcelona)* regularly draws strips for Spain's popular *El Vibora.* His book *The Cabbie* (Catalan) has been published in English.

190 THE THINKERS. *Richard McGuire (nyc)* contributes illustrations to *The Village Voice* and *NY Times,* designs flip books, and creates mechanical toys.

191 THE SMELL OF SHALLOW GRAVES. *Charles Burns (philadelphia)* will be designing sets for the Mark Morris/Monnaie Dance production of the *Nutcracker Suite.*

Back cover illustration © 1984/90 Gary Panter

88 PP   10 1/2" x 14 1/8" **$15**

20" x 27" **$14.95**

204 PP   6" x 8 3/4" **$14.95**

160 PP   6" x 9" **$9.95**

68 PP   8 1/2" x 11" **$5.95**

RAW PRODUCT

READ YOURSELF RAW: The rare first three issues of RAW have been reprinted by Pantheon Books in their original large format complete with color covers, City of Terror gum cards and Two-Fisted Painters, a color insert book...Joost Swarte's cover for RAW, Vol. 1, No. 2, has been published as a full-color offset **POSTER** promoting the RAW/Pantheon books...All back issues of RAW are out of print, except for **RAW Vol. 2, No. 1,** which includes Charles Burns' epic "Teen Plague," Chapter 8 of MAUS, full color commix by Swarte, Beyer, Mattotti, and Loustal, and much more...The first 6 chapters of art spiegelman's MAUS have been published by Pantheon as **MAUS, A Survivor's Tale**...Ben Katchor has edited and published **PICTURE STORY No. 2,** featuring commix by himself and Mark Beyer as well as color paintings from Jerry Moriarty's Visual Crimes series ...Mark Beyer chronicles the multiple deaths of Amy and Jordan in **AGONY** ($7.95), a Big Little Book for adults...Charles Burns' razor sharp brush delineates five adventures of El Borbah, a 400 pound private eye in **HARD-BOILED DEFECTIVE STORIES** ($8.95)...**JIMBO** ($12.95) features Gary Panter's punk hero in new stories and earlier adventures as they appeared in RAW...The new three-color RAW lapel **BUTTON** ($1.50) features Gary Panter's cover for RAW Vol. 2, No. 1... All these books and many more are available from Catalan Communications, which is now handling all our mail orders...

ORDERING INFO

NY orders add 8.25% tax. Postage & Handling, add $2 per book and $2.50 for up to 5 posters/prints (no charge for orders of 6 or more books or posters). Canadian/Foreign: add $5 on book orders, $2.50 for posters. Payment in US dollars only.

CATALAN COMMUNICATIONS
43 East 19th, NYC, NY 10003.
Phone: (212) 254-4996

IT WAS THE BIG DINNER OF OUR WHOLE FAMILY. ALL MY COUSINS, AUNTS AND UNCLES, AND THE LUDERMYERS FROM NEXT DOOR CARRIED IN FOOD, FOOD, FOOD.

TEN MILLION TONS OF FOOD WRAPPED IN ALCOA AND SARAN WRAP. THEN, BEFORE WE COULD EAT, MR. LUDERMYER MADE A TOAST TO MY DAD.

THE PARTY WAS FOR HIM QUITTING DRINKING. MY GRANDMA STARTED CRYING AND HUGGING MY DAD. SHE KEPT GIVING ME AND MY SISTER THE SIGNAL TO CRY AND HUG OUR DAD TOO.

SHE KEPT GIVING OUR UNCLE JOHN THE SIGNAL TO TAKE THE PICTURES AND MY AUNT WILDA KEPT GIVING THE SIGNAL FOR EVERYONE ELSE TO QUIT STARING AND START EATING.

AFTER DINNER EVERYBODY SAT OUT IN THE BACKYARD LISTENING TO MOSTLY MR. LUDERMYER TALKING.

MY GRANDMA SAID DAD OWED HIS LIFE TO THAT MAN. MR. LUDERMYER WHO HELPED HIM OUT. MR. LUDERMYER WHO GAVE HIM THAT JOB.

I WATCHED HOW MR. LUDERMYER KEPT PUTTING HIS ARM AROUND MY DAD AND HOW MY DAD KEPT DRINKING MORE PEPSI, MORE PEPSI, MORE PEPSI.

THEN MY DAD STOOD UP AND PULLED OUT HIS CAR KEYS. "WHERE YOU GOING, RAY?" MY GRANDMA SAID. "CIGARETTES" MY DAD SAID.

"CHRIST, I MAY AS WELL COME WITH YOU" MR. LUDERMYER SAID. "BLOW THE DUST OFF OF ME." HE WAS GIVING MY GRANDMA A LOOK.

"NAW" SAID MY DAD. "I'LL BE RIGHT BACK" MY GRANDMA STOOD UP. "BRING THE KIDS WITH YOU, RAY." SHE SAID.

BUT HE WAS ALREADY DOWN THE DRIVEWAY. ALREADY DOWN THE DARK STREET.

TWO HOURS AFTER MY DAD STILL WASN'T BACK, MY AUNT WILDA STARTED SLAMMING THINGS AROUND IN THE KITCHEN.

WHERE'D HE GO FOR CIGARETTES, TIMBUKTU?

DOES HE THINK WE'RE IDIOTS?

I KNOW DAMN WELL WHERE HE IS.

WRAP!

"HE DOESN'T THINK OF ANYONE BUT HIMSELF" SHE SAID. "NEVER HAS AND NEVER WILL." SHE GOT HER BOWLS AND YELLED FOR HER KIDS TO GET THEIR COATS ON.

YOU SHUSH. YOU DON'T KNOW—

—OH DON'T I?

COME ON MOM. JESUS CHRIST.

EVERYONE WAS LEAVING. PRETTY SOON IT WAS JUST MY GRANDMA AND MR. LUDERMYER SITTING IN THE KITCHEN.

BELIEVE ME, NOLA. I KNOW EXACTLY HOW YOU FEEL.

GOT ANY MORE OF THAT CAKE HANDY?

I SAT ON THE BACK PORCH WITH MY LITTLE SISTER. SHE TOLD ME SHE WAS FEELING KIND OF SICK. I THOUGHT SHE WAS FAKING TO GET ATTENTION BUT THEN SHE THREW UP.

GRANDMA!

IN A WAY HER BARFING TURNED OUT TO BE A GOOD THING BECAUSE IT MADE MY GRANDMA COME RUNNING OUT AND IT TOOK HER MIND OFF MY DAD.

YES. YES. IT'S OK, HONEY. COME ON INSIDE.

YOU GONNA BE OK?

THE BAD PART ABOUT IT WAS IT MEANT I GOT STUCK WITH MR. LUDER-MYER WHO STARTED TO GIVE ME HIS PHILOSOPHY ON LIFE.

LET A SMILE BE YOUR UMBRELLA.

THAT ABOUT SAYS IT ALL, DOESN'T IT?

HE STARTED SAYING HIS OBSERVATIONS ABOUT BEING A GOOD FATHER AND I ABOUT SAID IF YOU'RE SO PERFECT, HOW COME YOUR DAUGHTER IS ABOUT THE BIGGEST SLUT AT OUR SCHOOL?

AND I'VE HEARD MANY WORDS IN MY DAY BUT NONE AS BEAUTIFUL AS "I LOVE YOU DADDY"

AND RIGHT THEN CINDY LUDERMYER COMES OUT ON THEIR BACK PORCH AND SAYS "DAD. COME ON DAD. IT'S LATE." CINDY LUDERMYER AND ME HATE EACH OTHER.

DAD!

MR. LUDERMYER SAYS "IN A MINUTE, HONEY" AND THEN HE LOOKS AT ME LIKE THERE'S A MOVIE DOING A CLOSE UP OF HIS FACE ABOUT THE BEAUTY OF LIFE, AND ALL I CAN THINK IS: "YOU ARE SO STUPID."

THE TIME HAS COME...

FOR US TO PART

YEAH. GOODNIGHT.

THE ONLY REASON CINDY LUDERMYER WANTS HIM TO COME IN AND GO TO SLEEP IS BECAUSE SHE'S SNEAKING OUT TONIGHT.

EVERYONE IS. MY COUSIN ROYLTON JAMES SAID MEET AT THE ROPE SWING AT 2AM. BRING JUNGLE JUICE.

YOUR SISTER'S ASLEEP. DON'T YOU DARE WAKE HER.

OK. GOODNIGHT. GRANDMA.

AND DON'T FORGET YOUR PRAYERS.

JUNGLE JUICE IS WHEN YOU KYPE INCHES OF EVERY KIND OF BOOZE AND MIX IT IN ONE JAR. THERE WASN'T ANY BOOZE IN MY GRANDMAS HOUSE. AND I DIDN'T KNOW IF I EVEN FELT LIKE GOING ANYWAY.

WITH MY HYPERTENSION, I WON'T MAKE IT THROUGH THE NIGHT.

WE GOT TO FIND HIM.

NO. THE KIDS ARE SLEEPING. THEY'LL BE FINE.

MY COUSIN ROYLTON JAMES WAS STANDING SOAKING WET IN HIS UNDERWEAR DRINKING OUT OF A BOY SCOUT CANTEEN.
PATTY HERZOCK WAS HANGING OFF THE ROPE SWING IN HER BRA AND PANTIES

YOU GUYS!

HEY! I SAID SOME ONE PULL ME IN!

JUST JUMP!

IT'S *TOO* COLD! COME ON!

CHICKEN!!

DAN AND RON GLYNN WERE THERE AND DORIS BELL AND MARY HURLEY. EVERYONE WAS IN THEIR UNDERWEAR. MY COUSIN YELLED "SKINNY DIP!" WHEN HE SAW US. PATTY HERZOCK DROPPED OFF THE ROPE SWING AND CAME UP SCREAMING.

"BYE" CINDY SAID TO ME AND RAN OVER TO DAN GLYNN AND JUMPED ON HIS BACK. A RADIO WAS PLAYING. A SONG ABOUT "IF HER DADDY'S RICH" AND DAN STARTED SINGING IT TO CINDY.

HEY HOG GIVE ME SOME!

THEN A GUY, TOM DONATO PUT HIS ARM AROUND ME AND GAVE ME SOME DRINKS OF HIS JUNGLE JUICE.

CINDY LUDERMYER MADE A BIG DEAL ABOUT TAKING OFF HER CLOTHES AND EVERYONE GOT QUIET WATCHING HER. CINDY'S NICKNAME WAS "THE BOD."

ROYLTON!

DANNY!

TOMMY!

RONNY!

YOU GUYS QUIT STARIN'

I WAS DRUNK AND EVERYONE WAS DRUNK. TOM DONATO STARTED FRENCHING ME AND WHEN I LOOKED AROUND, EVERYONE WAS FRENCHING EVERYONE ELSE.

"COME ON" TOM SAID. WE WENT BACK DEEPER IN THE WOODS. WE DRANK MORE JUNGLE JUICE AND WE WERE LAYING DOWN. STICKS AND BRANCHES WERE STICKING ME IN THE BACK.

HE KEPT TAKING MY HAND AND PUTTING IT IN HIS UNDERWEAR. I KEPT NOT DOING IT. HE KEPT SAYING "PLEASE, PLEASE" AND FINALLY I TOUCHED IT FOR ABOUT ONE MINUTE THEN HE SAT UP AND BARFED.

I ABOUT STARTED BARFING TOO. I COULD HARDLY WALK. I WENT OVER TO FIND MY COUSIN AND I STARTED CRYING FOR NO REASON AND TOLD ROYLTON TOM USED ME.

THEN I CAN'T HARDLY REMEMBER. SOME-ONE WAS FEELING ME UP AND I WAS CRYING. CINDY LUDERMYER WAS CRYING TOO BECAUSE SHE BARFED OUT HER RETAINER AND COULDN'T FIND IT.

AND THEN ALL OF A SUDDEN I WAS ON THE FOOT BRIDGE TRYING TO WALK HOME. IT WAS STARTING TO GET LIGHT. I WAS TALKING TO GOD OUT LOUD, TELLING HIM TO PLEASE JUST LET ME GET HOME.

IN THE A+W PARKING LOT I SAW MY DAD'S CAR. I TRIED CUTTING AROUND THE OTHER WAY BUT HE CAUGHT ME. "HI DAD." I SAID AND I THREW UP.

HE TOOK ME TO A GAS STATION BATH-ROOM AND TOLD ME TO CLEAN UP. "IF YOUR GRANDMA SEES YOU LIKE THIS, SHE'LL GO APE SHIT" HE SAID. WHEN I CAME OUT HE HANDED ME COFFEE. MY FIRST CUP OF COFFEE.

"WE'RE BOTH IN THE DOGHOUSE" HE SAID. AND HE DIDN'T ASK ME NOTHING AND I DIDN'T ASK HIM NOTHING. EXCEPT HE DID ASK ME IF I SMOKED. AND HE DID GIVE ME A CIGARETTE.

WE SAT IN THE CAR. HE TOLD ME WORK-ING FOR MR. LUDERMYER WAS KILLING HIM AND LIVING WITH GRANDMA WAS DRIVING HIM NUTS. I KNEW HE WAS LEAVING AGAIN. I KNEW IT.

IT WASN'T THE FIRST TIME HE LEFT AND IT WASN'T THE LAST TIME HE LEFT. HE SAID HE WAS GLAD I UNDERSTOOD. I COULDN'T SAY ANYTHING.

I'M LUCKY I GOT A KID LIKE YOU.

NO, LISTEN. I AM.

WHEN HE DROPPED ME OFF, HE TOLD ME THREE THINGS. TELL GRANDMA NOT TO WORRY, TELL MY SISTER HE LOVED HER, AND FOR ME TO CHEW ASPIRIN FOR MY HANGOVER.

BE GOOD. AND DON'T GIVE YOUR GRANDMA NO TROUBLE.

AND WHEN HIS CAR PULLED AWAY, I TURNED AROUND AND SAW MY GRANDMA AND MR. LUDERMYER STANDING IN THE PICTURE WINDOW.

THE BASKET CASE

I was finally coming home after too many years of horror and fear.

I just wanted one thing: to forget.

I went back to the building I'd left so dramatically four years ago.

The hall stank of urine. It was comforting.

Translated by Robert Legault, Kim Thompson, F.M. & a.s. Lettering by Paul Karasik.

I felt no joy looking over the seedy piles of trash I used to love. The apartment smelled moldy and the electricity had been shut off. The place felt alien to me and I couldn't stay there another minute. I decided to go out right away.

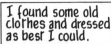
I found some old clothes and dressed as best I could.

I felt lousy, but I thought my vague fears would disappear as soon as I got out.

But...

DRRIIINNG

Ah! So there you are, Mr. Choumacher...

I've been comin' to yer door every day at this time fer two years. I was startin' to think you wasn't comin' back... You were real lucky to get out in one piece, Mr. Choumacher. Let's go light a candle to some Saint and say Hallelujah...

The guy talked and talked... But I'd forgotten how to listen. When he finally shut up, I'd completely lost track of whatever he was saying. He handed me an envelope and disappeared.

I stuffed it in my pocket, gave him a few minutes lead, and stepped outside.

I drowned myself in alcohol for most of the night. When I finally came up for air, it was too late: she was there.

She wanted me to go with her. Her arguments were very convincing and I didn't resist.

We paused a few times in the middle of the street, in neighborhoods I'd never seen before. During one of those pauses, I was gripped by a deep anxiety. If I hadn't been so totally confused, I could have tried to avoid the worst-- though thinking back on it now, I'm sure it was already too late.

The electricity had been cut off when I got home. But still, the old guy with the envelope was able to ring the doorbell... I couldn't get that fact out of my head.

5

Not only did she know it, she used it.

M..MOUH

? MOUH

Stay here! I'll be right back...

You jerk! You're making one hell of a mistake...

MM M MH

7

I didn't understand any of this, but I should have: it was pretty clear but I was in no condition to figure it out. Instead of thinking, I just got boiling mad.

It's time for you to go now.

I'm sick of this shit! If you brought me here just to make fun of me, shove it! I'm getting really pissed off!

Get your ass over here!

You think you're so smart, but you're just as stupid as all the others... all the others with their big dicks!

She didn't resist at all: quite the opposite....she let me do anything I wanted. That should have ripped me off.

I panicked. I didn't think I could commit such acts, but I soon started to question this vague conviction and began to feel pangs of guilt.

And I thought about how those last four years of extreme humiliation had been more than enough to turn me into a monster.

That's when I found the envelope in my pocket. Inside: a piece of paper, an address.

I wandered through parts of Paris I'd never been in before.

Going to the address in the old guy's envelope never even occurred to me.

As I staggered through the streets, horror seemed to leap at me from every corner.

Then I found myself in front of my building.

I couldn't resist. I went up to my place.

By now it was clear that I was caught inside a monstrous trap.

The scream came from a closet I didn't even know existed in my own apartment.

Ah... it's you, Choumacher. Come in!

The old guy with the envelope was inside. I was doomed.

Don't make a scene!

I was scared, but I knew the score. Whatever happened to me now didn't matter much.

It had to come sooner or later.

Take him, boys! Gently!

The French police used their time-honored methods that had earned them their reputation.

Finally, I had some peace.

The trial was an ordeal for me. The only thing I remember is trying to get some credit for medals I was given for crawling through the mud, but it did no good.

The death penalty was pronounced.

One morning around 3 A.M., they treated me to a glass of wine and a cigarette. I even put up with confession and the prison chaplain leaning over me. I had nothing left to lose.

Funny thing: I still thought I'd get out of it.

The early morning air didn't make me feel any better; just the opposite. I relieved myself in my pants, so that a nasty smell surrounded us. 19

We walked past the Municipal Guards whose uniforms looked just like the one I wore at the beginning of what was to be my downfall.

NO!

OH...

I remember it all, as if it were yesterday.

22

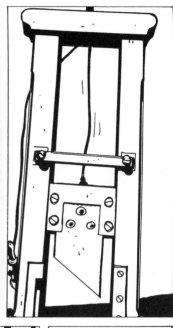

Hey, the bastard doesn't wanna croak! The blade's stuck. Pull it up again, George.

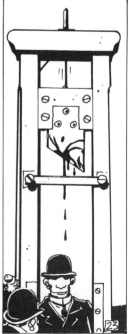

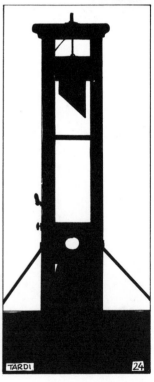

Pictures by
SUE COE

Text by
ANDREW TYLER

THIS LITTLE PIGGY
WENT TO MARKET

MEAT FOR BEGINNERS

Most of us would prefer not to think about where the meat we eat comes from, but if pressed, we would picture a farm, a larger version of the one in our childhood books, with cows in a pasture, pigs wallowing in a pen and chickens in a hen house. Nine chances out of ten we're wrong. Age-old practices have been supplanted without fanfare over the past forty years, and nowadays the slab of meat we pick from the supermarket cooler will almost certainly have been produced through what is known as "factory," "confinement," or "intensive" farming.

DURING and after World War II, the high demand for poultry and eggs led feed and pharmaceutical companies to attempt to solve the problems inherent in large-scale production of chickens. The discovery that vitamins A and D added to feed could substitute for exercise and sunlight had led to early experiments where large flocks were crowded in cramped buildings. But many farmers were ruined when contagious diseases wiped out their entire "production."[1] It was soon discovered that antibiotics not only controlled the diseases, but also accelerated the chickens' weight gain. In 1981, after more than 30 years of routinely feeding antibiotics to animals, a technical service consultant for American Cyanamid (a company which produced $120 million worth of antibiotics for animal use in the US and $265 million abroad that year) could still be quoted as saying: "Frankly, we don't quite know how or why they work."[2]

IN THE early factory farms, another problem literally piled up: chicken shit. That led to the confinement of the birds in wire cages, the droppings falling on conveyor belts, automated as were the feeding, watering, light and ventilation systems. Soon the crowded cages were stacked two and three rows high in buildings holding tens of thousands of chickens.

AN ENTIRE life spent standing on metal wires an inch apart produces multiple foot and body malformations, but chickens that would live up to 15 or 20 years when raised free-range are now sent to slaughter after eight weeks, before the malformations affect the carcass. The intense crowding and unrelieved boredom lead to what the industry demurely calls "stress." Raising animals in total darkness except at feeding times alleviates some of the symptoms. The thousands of 'broilers' raised together cannot begin to establish the pecking order that instinct would make them develop in the barnyard. Stress and uncontrolled pecking introduced the new problem of cannibalism, which was resolved by the Debeaker, a machine that slices off the beak of newly-hatched chickens with a hot blade. Similarly, to prevent severely stressed pigs from eating each other's rumps, the tails and needle teeth of piglets are cut off as soon as they are born.[1]

MANY animals die of mysterious new ailments clearly brought about by stress and confinement. Poultry's "flip-over syndrome" is "characterized by birds jumping into the air, sometimes emitting a loud squawk and then falling over dead."[1] Intensive farming itself has made their lives very cheap indeed. In hatcheries producing "egg-type" birds, males, the useless half of the chicks, are simply

thrown in garbage bags to suffocate, and then fed to minks.

BY THE mid 60's, techniques developed for the factory farming of poultry were extended to pigs, cattle and sheep. It is estimated that now 70% of hogs and 90% of egg-laying hens are raised in total-confinement systems. The few remaining farmers may not survive the competition from agribusiness much longer. Though the profits are huge (the meat industry is the second largest manufacturing and processing concern in the US), the costs to the environment and to consumers are even greater.

DOMESTICATED ruminants (cattle, sheep, goats) used to play a positive role in a man-controlled ecology. They can digest cellulose otherwise undigestible to man and other animals and fertilize the soil with their manure. Now most cattle, raised in feedlots, are fed a high-grain diet which gets them "finished" (fattened for slaughter) faster and produces the more tender "marbled" meat preferred by the consumer. Through this practice, cattle directly compete with humans for food and consume 50% of the world's grain production (while wasting 90% of its protein). This allows author John Robbins to say in *Diet for a New America*[3] that the 60 million people who will starve to death this year could be adequately fed by the grain saved if Americans reduced their meat consumption by 10% (although obviously this assumes that the meat industry would donate valuable cattle fodder to humans).

STILL, cattle need roughage for their digestive systems to function properly. In this alienated world of hi-tech farming, traditional hay is now often replaced by "exotic feeds," which include plastic hay (pellets made of 80-90% ethylene and 10-20% propylene), peanut skins, reject junk food, sawdust, bark, cement dust, chicken shit, feathers, newspapers, waste paper, and cardboard scraps. "We have a helluva time when these metal staples end up in our feed. It's not so bad for the big milk cows. You can drop a cow magnet into their stomachs and pick up all the bits of baling wire, staples and other hardware they might have eaten. But the young cows can't take it. Cuts them all up."[2]

THE LARGE scale of modern animal farming is at the root of some of its most dire consequences. Over 90% of *all* agricultural land—over half of the total land area of the US—is used for livestock agriculture, losing over 2 billion tons of soil every year.[4] US livestock produces 250,000 pounds of excrement each second,[3] and that manure is the cause of 90% of the water pollution in this country. In the US, as in the rest of the world, the conversion of forest land to grazing land is the major cause of deforestation.[4]

THE COMBINATION of cheaper meat with higher average income has made the consumption of meat per capita in the US triple between 1910 and 1970 while the consumption of grain and cereals was cut in half. Up to a point, increasing income did result in an improvement of the diet, but the low nutritional quality of the contemporary American diet (especially too much saturated fat from animal products) is the leading cause of cardiovascular disease, stroke, and many other "diseases of affluence." Whereas the average risk of death from a heart attack for a man in the US is 50%, it is only 15% for someone who doesn't eat meat and 4% for a pure "vegan" who eats no animal products at all.[3]

BESIDES their own "natural" saturated fat, meat and dairy products also provide us with 78% of the pesticides we ingest.[4] Then there's the question of hormones. DES, a synthetic estrogen, was extensively used as a growth promotant in livestock for 30 years. It was banned in 1979 after being proven carcinogenic in humans.[2] Though the effects on humans of other hormones have not been assessed, the European Community was wary enough to recently ban all US beef produced with them.

THE ANTIBIOTICS that made confinement farming possible (55% of all antibiotics used yearly in the US[3]) may create the greatest problem of all. To the surprise of scientists, by the end of the 60's, epidemics caused by antibiotic-resistant bacteria were being reported around the world. Studies have since shown that bacteria can acquire multiple resistance to antibiotics and that they can pass that resistance on to other bacteria.[2] "Unless we put a halt to the prodigal use of antibiotics and synthetic drugs, we may soon be forced back into a pre-antibiotic era."[5]

IN SWEDEN, production costs of raising animals did not appreciably increase after laws prohibiting the use of antibiotics were passed.[6] A 1978 study by the US Senate's Agricultural Committee shows that, though a prohibition on antibiotics would make confinement production systems less viable, small farmers would benefit, as it would encourage farm expansion for a few years, after which production and prices would level off.[1]

MEANWHILE back at the ranch, E. F. "Bud" Loats, central-regional manager of Cyanamid's Animal Industry Department, explains the thoughtful attitude that prevails in today's open frontier: "I'm not sure what all the ruckus over drug resistance is about. I mean, you've got these animals on drugs in their feed. Then five months after they're weaned, they're on a truck. Then they arrive at the packing plant and—boom!—they're gone. That's the end of that."[2]

SOURCES AND RECOMMENDED READING:
1. Jim Mason & Peter Singer, *Animal Factories*, (Crown Pub., 1980.)
2. Orville Schell, *Modern Meat*, (Random House, 1984.)
3. John Robbins, *Diet For a New America*, (Stillpoint Publishing, 1987.)
4. Fact sheet compiled by the Vegetarian Society of DC, PO Box 4921, Washington, DC 20008.
5. Dr. Tsutomo Watanabe, *Scientific American*, December 1987.
6. "The World's Meat Industry," *Meat and Poultry*, February 1989.

Baby pigs can be castrated any time after they are a week old. The baby boars should be herded out of the sow's pen. Mama sows can get very angry at such human "attacks" on their babies. Often the first squeals cause a nice, quiet, pet sow to leap up to the defense, looking like a savage tiger. Be careful.

Have your helper grab a pig by the hind feet, holding it upside down, with its belly towards you. Using the soapy water, scrub the area just in front of the scrotum. Dry the area. With your left hand push the testicles forward as far as they will comfortably go. This is where the incision is made, right over one testicle, still held bulging against the skin. The incision should run lengthwise (head to tail) and be about an inch long. Squeeze the testicle quite hard, and it will pop out of the incision.

If it will not come out, deepen the incision, and it will. Don't cut it off. Instead firmly grasp the testicle and cord and firmly pull until it comes free. Push the other testicle against the same incision and gently cut against it. Again, squeeze it, and it will pop out and be ready to pull free.

If there is any ragged tissue hanging from the incision, either pull it free or trim it off. Splash the incision with disinfectant and release the pig. With practice, this process is very easy.

—Raising Animals for Fun and Profit, *Tab Books, 1984.*

I had spent the morning at a South of England slaughterhouse watching truckloads of pigs getting briskly slaughtered and was returning home when our bus was halted by a funeral procession. Looking down from the top deck I could see the hearse with its polished coffin and gleaming brass rails, the half dozen other hired limousines and, beyond them, a string of family cars. Three or four solemn figures in black stepped out and conferred. They seemed lost, pointing this way and that. Then they climbed back in and the cortege slowly made off, our bus and the rest of the afternoon's traffic sucked along by default.

I'd seen three hundred pigs go down that morning, creatures known in vivisection circles as

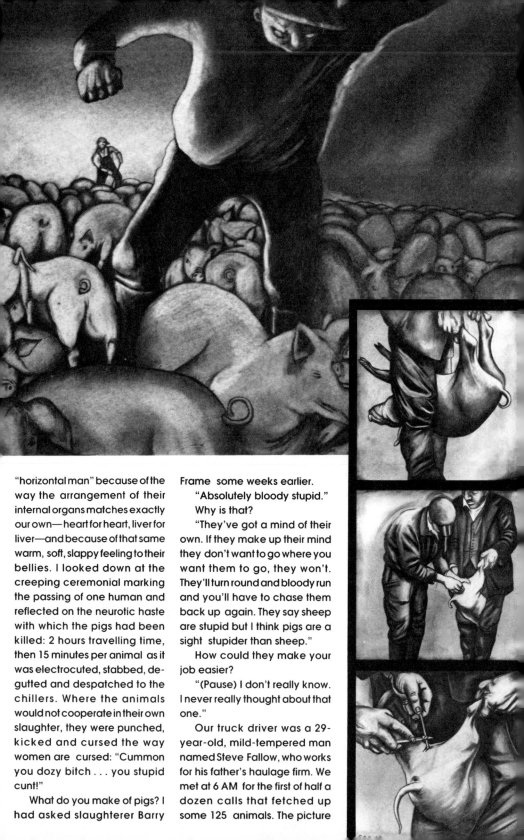

"horizontal man" because of the way the arrangement of their internal organs matches exactly our own—heart for heart, liver for liver—and because of that same warm, soft, slappy feeling to their bellies. I looked down at the creeping ceremonial marking the passing of one human and reflected on the neurotic haste with which the pigs had been killed: 2 hours travelling time, then 15 minutes per animal as it was electrocuted, stabbed, de-gutted and despatched to the chillers. Where the animals would not cooperate in their own slaughter, they were punched, kicked and cursed the way women are cursed: "Cummon you dozy bitch . . . you stupid cunt!"

What do you make of pigs? I had asked slaughterer Barry Frame some weeks earlier.

"Absolutely bloody stupid."

Why is that?

"They've got a mind of their own. If they make up their mind they don't want to go where you want them to go, they won't. They'll turn round and bloody run and you'll have to chase them back up again. They say sheep are stupid but I think pigs are a sight stupider than sheep."

How could they make your job easier?

"(Pause) I don't really know. I never really thought about that one."

Our truck driver was a 29-year-old, mild-tempered man named Steve Fallow, who works for his father's haulage firm. We met at 6 AM for the first of half a dozen calls that fetched up some 125 animals. The picture drawn by pigmen is of a cussed animal that refuses to abbreviate the passage from its mother's teat to the breakfast plate. But even the many farmers I've visited, who in the main kept their animals in a deep crust of unattended shit and urine, confining the breeding females to crates and stalls for the greater part of their lives that allowed scarcely the room to sink to the ground, subjecting them to a constant cycle of pregnancies; even they will admit that the pig, if permitted, is a clean animal who'll strain to deposit its waste well away from its living area; also a good mother with a talent for nest building; resourceful, physically powerful, unusually sensitive

and, yes, with an appetite, sharpened by the tedium of life-long confinement, as voracious as our own.

Pigs, Fallow tells me when we've set off, are happiest when traveling at a steady pace in

temperate weather. During the summer, particularly when the truck stops, they scramble furiously over one another to reach the air vents. Being unable to sweat, their body temperature soars. They also pile up in the winter, to keep warm. Either way, deaths often occur from heart attack or suffocation; the bodies are then deposited in pet food bins at the other end. Nothing but the squeal escapes.

I hear the scrambling as we drift past groups of forest ponies suckling their mothers in the middle of the road. By 9 AM we're at the abattoir, a unit on an industrial estate that looks, from its bland exterior, like any other. No sign declares the name or nature of business, and it is a condition of my entry that I withhold the firm's identity. Suffice it to say it is one of Southern England's largest, disposing of some 1,500 pigs weekly; EEC-licensed and therefore regarded as being superior to the majority of the other 1,000 odd UK operations.

Nothing but the squeal escapes.

He was dumped in a tank of freezing water, hoisted 15 feet and had power hoses trained on him.

"The thing that appealed to me when I first looked at it," a 22-year-old ex-slaughterman, now in the army, told me, "is that you got a lot of blokes working together and they're working fast and hard and you think 'Christ, I'd like to have a go at that' because they all look so hard, like they can definitely look after themselves. And they can because it's a very, very tough job to do."

Tough work, tough ritual, tough play-fights that, this man recalls, usually ended with the chaps love-biting each other. After his first week, he was dumped in a tank of freezing water, hoisted 15 feet and had power hoses trained on him. He was in. But that was a caress compared to what a colleague got during an idle moment. They penned him in a cow crush, ripped off his overalls and prodded him with electric tongs while dowsing him in water. When he got out he was carried, almost naked, down the yard and thrown in a tangle of gorse bushes. "He was cut to pieces," says his former colleague. And no, "not because he was unpopular... just for a joke." This is the nature of the regime our pigs entered.

The first thing that probably strikes them is the noise, in some locations like a roaring mechanical tide, elsewhere the explosive sound of metallic slamming and clanking, chains and hooks coupling and uncoupling, the hiss of power hoses, the bang of the "captive bolt" as it penetrates the skulls of cattle,

and mingling throughout, the shrieks of terror from doomed beasts.

Then they'd notice how the air is heavy with a demonic mist, a mixture of blood and foul water. It splashes and froths up from the bleeding troughs where animals are hung by a back leg after their throats are cut. And it washes in great black waves from the scalding tank as each newly slaughtered pig is dumped in.

Then there are the men—in their red and blue overalls, rubber aprons and hard hats; some of them with scabbards of knives, their forearms bared, blood splattering over their faces as they carve into the still twitching corpses. The blood covers their hands, wrists, up to their elbows. Even the meat inspectors, garbed in official white, are blood-splashed. It's in their hair and eyelashes, on the clipboards on which they note incidence of disease.

All the animals start in the "lairage," a large stone area divided by bar gates into a system of pens. From here cattle are driven single-file into the stunning box, a walled-in area 15 feet square, into which about a dozen animals at a time are corralled and shot through the skull, one at a time. They receive what the plant manager calls "electrical stimulation" of the brain. The manager has just such a phrase for every aspect of the killing process. He talks droningly of it, making it sound not merely commonplace but dull. The "stimulation" is accomplished by a pair of hand operated

tongs, like giant pliers, that are clamped on either side of the pig's head just in front of the ears.

The stunner himself, Paul Hammond, is a lank, bony-faced man of 28, bearded, with one wayward eye and forearms tattooed with the Reaper and wreathed skulls. He's been 10 years in the craft but just 6 months here. He told me his tattoos—ubiquitous among the plant's slaughtermen—dated from the days when he rode and brawled with a local biker's club. That's when he met his wife Ruby, who also rode and still does. "Among me mates," she told me, "they thought 'ooh! how can he do that, he must have guts, he must be a bit tasty.' Except if they had him coming home covered in blood with bits of fat in his hair, that would put them off a bit."

The effect of his job on other men, notes Hammond, has been to get them to "stand back," especially in the early days when he would take his little trick items along to the pub and slap them on a table: an animal's eyeball, or its penis. "What seems to get into people's heads," he says, "is like 'I'd better watch him. He might start carving me up because if he can open up a pig and rip the guts out of that, what's he going to do to me?'"

Our truckload of pigs is being readied for opening. As the first

> *I'd better watch him. If he can open up a pig and rip the guts out of that, what's he going to do to me?*

dozen are driven into the stunning pen, one urinates on the trot and makes a screeching noise I hadn't heard before. Blood and mucus fly from his snout, the eyes close, the front legs stiffen and when Hammond opens the tongs he falls, like a log, on his side. He lies there, back legs kicking, as Hammond turns to the next candidate. Most huddle against the entrance with their rumps towards him, heads passively bowed, snout to snout. They wait quietly until Hammond clamps another and then a couple break from the huddle and sniff a fallen comrade.

He tells me that the tongs should be held on for a minimum of 7 seconds to ensure a proper stun before the throat is cut. But Hammond, urged on by his mates further along the slaughterline, is giving them $1\frac{1}{2}$ or less. ("If you were from the Ministry I'd have to do it longer.")

When he's stunned three or four, he shackles each of them with a chain around a back leg. They are then mechanically lifted and carried to an adjoining stone room where his col-

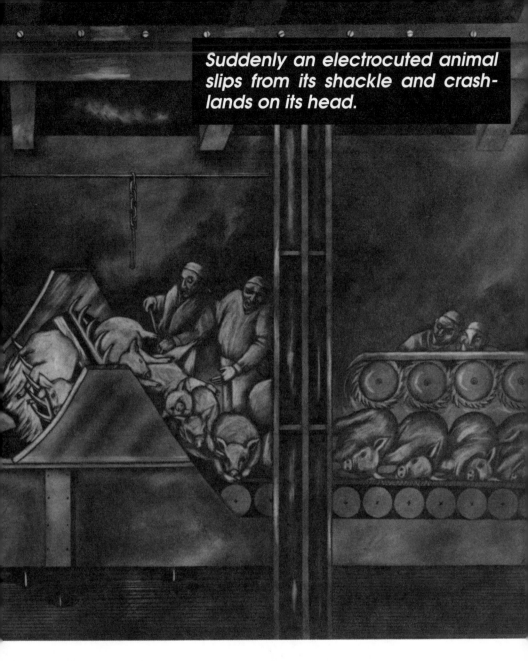

Suddenly an electrocuted animal slips from its shackle and crash-lands on its head.

league, Dave, cuts deep into the neck and the still pumping heart gushes out the blood. Hammond is supposed to stun and shackle one animal at a time since the delay involved in doing them in groups means they could go wide awake to the blade. The animals are probably conscious anyway given the 2-second stunning time he allows them.

Suddenly an electrocuted animal slips from its shackle en route to the sticking room, drops 5 feet to the stone floor and crash-lands on its head. Hammond continues jolting more creatures while the pig's back legs paddle furiously. Without re-stunning, he hooks it up again and sends it through to the knife. This crash landing routine is to be

repeated several more times in the next few minutes—caused by a combination of haste and incompetence, particularly on the part of Dave who takes over the shackling after a third man replaces him on the knife.

One animal slams down twice. Dave curses it as it lies paddling, blood seeping from anus and mouth. Hammond,

meanwhile, is ear wrestling a would-be escapee who is leaping at a small opening in the metal gate. "You can have it another fucking way then you idiot," Dave cries, as he helps slap the animal down.

The slaughtermen are prompted by the pressures to increase slaughterhouse throughput or else by the urge farmers feel to get injured animals to slaughter before they expire and become worthless. A young slaughterman tells me of a farmer who had dragged his cow, "its insides actually hanging out from a bad birth," to slaughter by hooking a hangman's noose around her neck and tieing the other end to a tractor. "He had literally peeled the skin from the base of its neck up behind the ears."

The same slaughterer tells me of the practitioner who, when faced with cattle unwilling to enter the killing box, would "stab their eyes so they couldn't see, then stick the boning knife actually in its arse, not in its back leg but its arse, to make it run forward."

It is interesting to note what still reaches a slaughterman's calloused heart—calloused, that is, by the work he's commissioned to do by the consumer. For one ex-slaughterman I spoke to it was young goats. "They cry just like babies." For a veteran blood and guts disposal man at the South of England plant it is carrying three-day-old calves to the shooting box and destroying them with a captive bolt. "I reckon it's wrong."

Paul Hammond, though, this morning's pig stunner, is unmoved while telling me about the day when, assisted by two other men, he shot 2,500 dis-

eased pigs on a farm, with women workers weeping for the younger piglets and the favored sows. "The way I look at it, if I can stop the disease spreading, that way it's not going to affect my livelihood and then I can carry on paying the bills."

He sounded similarly pragmatic when describing the swimming lessons some pigs get. "Sometimes if the chap sticking is rushing, he might not stick it right. It looks dead when

it's all hung up but you put it in the hot water tank and it ain't. It thrashes about. It will die eventually, probably drown in the tank."

The hot tank is the stage after the knife. Having bled over a long trough, the shackled ani-

mal, still kicking and writhing (an involuntary, autonomic response, say experts, even though these experts cannot agree about the onset of unconsciousness and death and when pain ceases) is elevated up a stone shaft, round a bend and

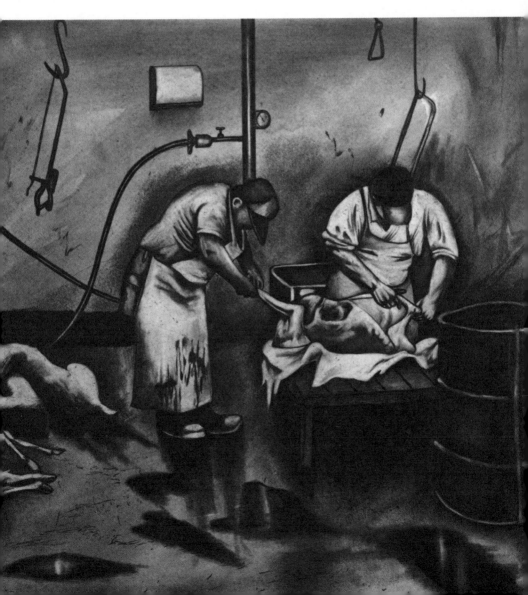

into the tank. The scene here is sheer medieval: three stooped men with long hooked poles, dark steam rising about them, bend over the tank in which seven or eight exsanguinated pigs are floating, eyes open.

They thrust them under the muddy, dung stained water and then onto a giant, half-submerged cradle constructed like a dinner fork minus the handle. This lifts them into a smaller adjoining tank in which they are briskly rotated and scraped of bristles.

Immediately beyond this, a dozen other men work in line converting the exsanguinated corpse into a product fit for the supermarket cooler. The swift-

ness of the operation is stunning, not least because the local authority inspectors, whose job is to look for tumorous and otherwise infected tissue, are encompassed by the tumult. As the pigs spin from the tank, two men shave them once more, another strikes out the toenails. They move down the line where the belly is opened and the guts pour out. These are slung onto a metal table and an inspector prods them for the likes of worms and lymph nodes. Reject material goes to the pet food bins. The rest slips down a chute to the gut room where it is partly untangled and readied for collection by the renderer, who'll sell it on for the manufacture of sausage skins,

diabetic insulin, and cosmetic products such as lipstick.

Meanwhile, the body has moved forward and is having its heart, liver and lungs removed, known collectively as "the pluck." A second inspector checks them for respiratory problems, notably pneumonia, which is widespread due to intensive production methods. Livers get afflicted less often by roundworm, and the heart quite frequently by an inflammation of the pericardium. The third check is of ribs, lungs and abdominal cavity for cases of pleurisy, peritonitis and TB. And then, about fifteen minutes after the tongs were applied, the extirpated beast is being carried down a level to be weighed, probed for fat ratio, stamped, chilled and trucked out.

If the ability of the local authority's meat inspectors to do a sound job is in serious doubt, then

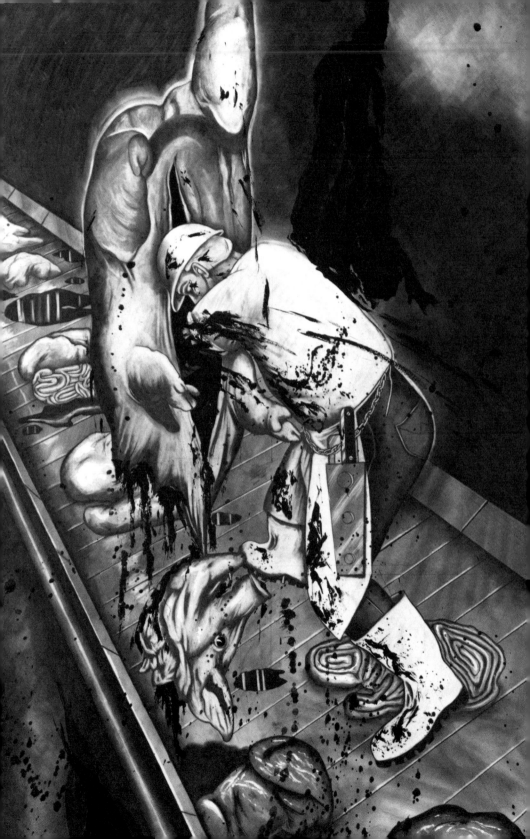

even more dubious are the twice-yearly hygiene and welfare checks by the Ministry of Agriculture vets, acting on behalf of the EEC.

"We had one the other day," says Hammond, "which totally fucks up our routine." Among the things they like to see is the proper stunning, shackling and 'sticking' of animals; that, for instance, the men don't sit about the canteen in blood-splashed slaughtering gear (which I saw them do) and that knives are properly sterilized between activities—so that the same unwashed blade isn't used to cut a dung and mud-stained hide as is used to cut into the tissue itself.

But Hammond thinks such routines are pointlessly time consuming and, thus, are ignored day to day. When the inspector comes, however, "you slow right down and do everything nice and properly and clean and tidy, which doesn't make an ha'pence of difference to the finished article. What's more, these blokes know it doesn't go on when they're not there. They only have to look at the graph of the weekly kill to see we're taking three times as long to do half the work."

As abattoirs go, this is not a rogue outfit but is regarded as top-notch and practicing "humane slaughter." And Ham-

mond is not an outrageous example but a typical and experienced practitioner. Says Hammond: "A cousin of mine asked, 'You don't actually kill them, do you?' So I said, 'What do you think we do, run round a field waiting for them to die?' People can be very small-minded."

I thought about his remark as I gazed on the funeral procession. Tolstoy, for one, believed we apply different ethical standards to men and animals at our peril. "As long as there are slaughterhouses there will be battlefields."

—Andrew Tyler

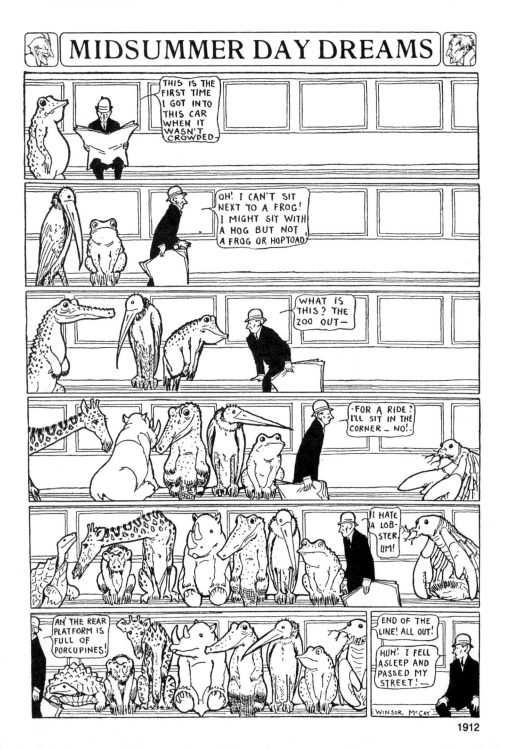

1912

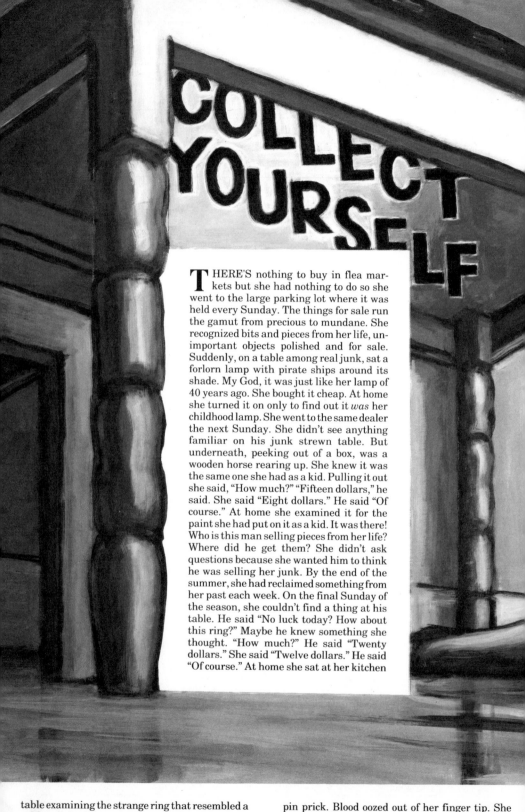

COLLECT YOURSELF

T HERE'S nothing to buy in flea markets but she had nothing to do so she went to the large parking lot where it was held every Sunday. The things for sale run the gamut from precious to mundane. She recognized bits and pieces from her life, unimportant objects polished and for sale. Suddenly, on a table among real junk, sat a forlorn lamp with pirate ships around its shade. My God, it was just like her lamp of 40 years ago. She bought it cheap. At home she turned it on only to find out it *was* her childhood lamp. She went to the same dealer the next Sunday. She didn't see anything familiar on his junk strewn table. But underneath, peeking out of a box, was a wooden horse rearing up. She knew it was the same one she had as a kid. Pulling it out she said, "How much?" "Fifteen dollars," he said. She said "Eight dollars." He said "Of course." At home she examined it for the paint she had put on it as a kid. It was there! Who is this man selling pieces from her life? Where did he get them? She didn't ask questions because she wanted him to think he was selling her junk. By the end of the summer, she had reclaimed something from her past each week. On the final Sunday of the season, she couldn't find a thing at his table. He said "No luck today? How about this ring?" Maybe he knew something she thought. "How much?" He said "Twenty dollars." She said "Twelve dollars." He said "Of course." At home she sat at her kitchen

table examining the strange ring that resembled a spider. It had a strange compartment that she tried to force open with her fingernail. She felt a pin prick. Blood oozed out of her finger tip. She sucked it. Within seconds she was writhing on the floor in convulsions. In a minute she was dead.

Next to her contorted face lay the ring, its compartment open. A small oval photo of her mother peered out... ❑

A VISUAL CRIME—NUMBER 7.
WRITTEN & ILLUSTRATED
BY JERRY MORIARTY

HE HAD A FUNNY FACE

©1989 **DREW FRIEDMAN**

JOPO DE POJO IN:

SWEET

A BOX OF BONBONS... YUM! I CAN'T WAIT TO TRY THEM. COME ON IN. POUR YOURSELVES A DRINK.

HE'S NOT SHARING THEM WITH HIS GUESTS. HE MUST REALLY LOVE THEM.

I'LL KEEP THIS UGLY BOX OUT OF SIGHT.

LATER AT THE NEIGHBORS

I CAN'T SLEEP WITH THAT RACKET NEXT DOOR. COULD IT BE A QUARREL?

MAYBE SOMEONE NEEDS OUR HELP.

IT SOUNDS LIKE A PARTY!

A PARTY? BAH... WHY WEREN'T WE INVITED?

WE REALLY HAVE TO GET HOME NOW. IF YOU WANT US TO HELP YOU CLEAN UP, DON'T BE AFRAID TO ASK.

DON'T WORRY I'LL MANAGE.

THANKS AGAIN, WE REALLY HAD A GOOD TIME.

BROKEN GLASSES, OVERFLOWING ASHTRAYS, HERE I COME.

Color assist by Supermarc Zanzibar

END

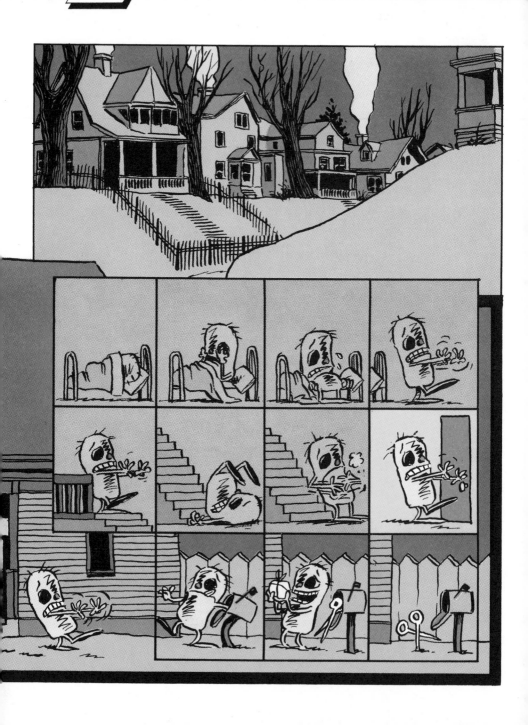

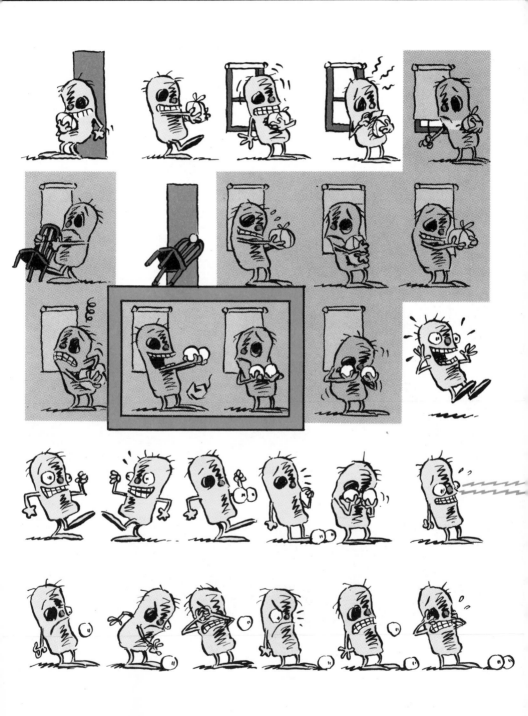

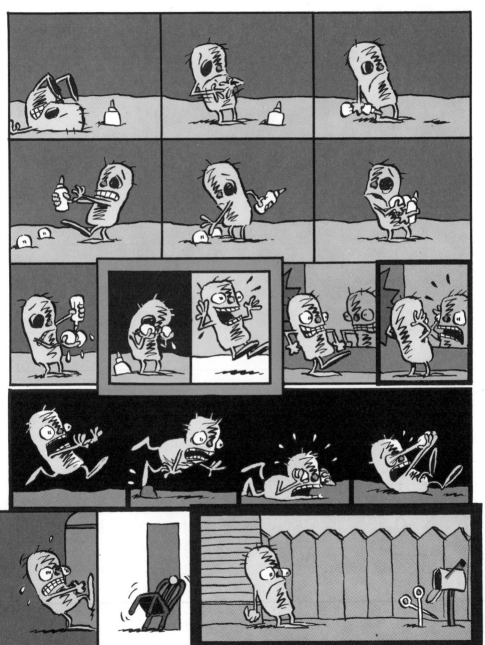

COWBOY HENK

EXCUSE ME, MA'AM, MAY I COME IN TO WIND UP MY WATCH?

DO YOU HAVE A SCREWDRIVER?

SHALL I HELP HIM?

YOU STAY IN BED, DEAR. YOU NEED INTENSIVE REST.

IS IT POSSIBLE TO GET A STRONG CUP OF COFFEE?

THESE GEARS ARE MORE RESISTANT THAN I THOUGHT!!

ZZZZZ

END

C O W B O Y   H E N K

TEN STEAKS, PLEASE...

SHALL I WRAP THEM UP, OR WILL YOU EAT THEM HERE?

EAT THEM?! NO WAY, I'M A VEGETARIAN...

...BUT BUTCHERS HAVE TO LIVE TOO, RIGHT?!

Translation by Anton VanDalen. Lettering by Jonathan Shapiro. Coloring by R.S. © 1989 Kamagurka/Herr Seele

OBA'S ELECTROPLATE FACTORY

by Yoshiharu Tsuge

THE OWNER OF OBA'S ELECTRO-PLATE FACTORY DIED OF TUBERCULOSIS A YEAR AGO.

ELECTROPLATE WORKERS OFTEN GET LUNG DISEASES

AFTER HE DIED ONLY TWO PEOPLE STAYED ON: HIS WIFE AND YOSHIO, A KID WHO'D ONLY BEEN THERE FOR SIX MONTHS. TOGETHER THEY BARELY GOT BY.

THE BOY EATS HIS LUNCH IN THE TINY ROOM WHERE THE OLD FOREMAN MR. KANEKO AND HIS FAMILY USED TO LIVE. IT FACES THE POND.

BEFORE OBA DIED
MR. KANEKO ALSO GOT
LUNG DISEASE. HE
HAD TO STOP WORKING.
THEY DIDN'T GIVE HIM
A PENSION, BUT THEY
LET HIS FAMILY
STAY IN THE
TINY ROOM.

MR. KANEKO'S WIFE WENT AROUND
SCAVENGING UP ANY LITTLE BITS
OF METAL SHE COULD FIND.

MR. KANEKO
WAS SO WEAK
THAT HE COULDN'T
STAND UP. HE SHAT
INTO THE POND
THROUGH A
HOLE IN
THE
FLOOR.

IT WASN'T JUST SHIT. IT WAS ALSO HIS ROTTING GUTS COMING OUT AND IT WASN'T JUST TUBERCULOSIS. IT WAS CHEMICAL POISONING IN HIS WHOLE BODY.

IT STINKS!

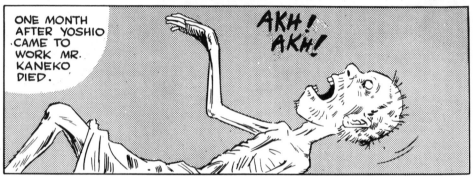

ONE MONTH AFTER YOSHIO CAME TO WORK MR. KANEKO DIED.

AKH! AKH!

KANEKO'S WIFE WASN'T THERE.

HE TRIED TO TALK TO HIS KIDS, BUT IT CAME OUT AS MOANS.

96

OF COURSE WE'LL MAKE MORE MONEY BY ELECTRO-PLATING.

BUT EVEN WITH THE EQUIPMENT YOU CAN'T DO ANYTHING WITHOUT SOME NICKEL AND CHROME.

YEAH. MRS. OBA HAD TO SELL THAT STUFF TO RAISE SOME CASH.

IF I TOLD YOU HOW MUCH THAT STUFF COSTS NOW IT'D MAKE YOUR EYEBALLS POP OUT.

THERE HAS BEEN A SHORTAGE OF NICKEL SINCE THE WAR IN KOREA STARTED.

WELL WE'VE JUST GOTTA EARN ENOUGH TO GET SOME.

DON'T WORRY I'LL FIND A WAY.

MR. MIYOSHI, A NEW JOB HAS COME IN.

FIRST YOU'VE GOT TO SOAK THEM IN POTASSIUM CYANIDE, THOUGH, TO TAKE THE RUST OFF.

ROGER!

BUSINESS IS SURE PICKING UP.

HEY, WE DON'T HAVE ANY POTASSIUM CYANIDE. WE'VE ONLY BEEN WORKING IN BRASS RECENTLY.

WELL, GO BUY A JUG OF IT.

WELL, I... I'M... I'M... UH...

I SEE... I'M BROKE, TOO.

WE CAN MAKE DO WITH TWO SMALL BOTTLES IF WE DILUTE IT.

* Editors' note: censored by artist for Japanese publication.

MY LEG'S ALL BETTER.

I DON'T THINK MRS. OBA AND MR. MIYOSHI ARE HOME.

WHA... WHAT ARE YOU DOING ALONE?

?

THEY LEFT IN THE DEAD OF THE NIGHT.

AND. YOU?

DEAD OF NIGHT ...

I HEARD THAT THEY WERE HEAVY IN DEBT.

SHE HAD TO SELL THE PLACE.

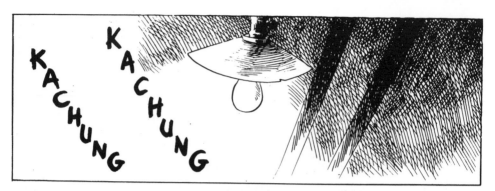

THE END

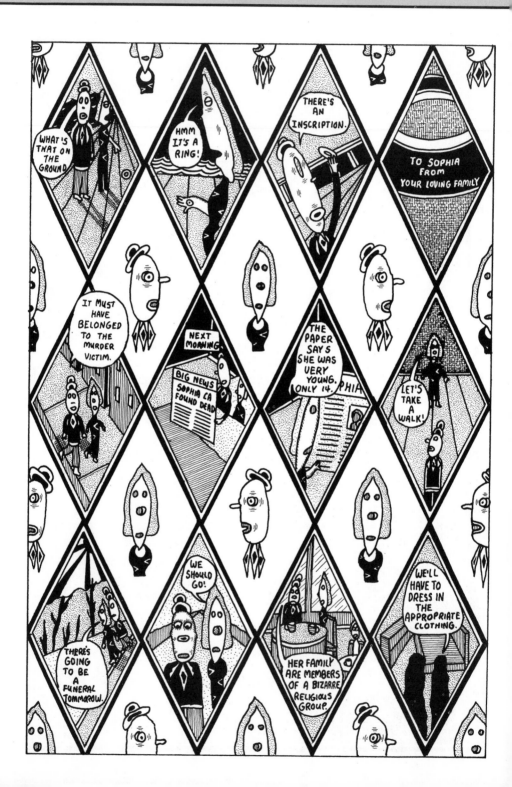

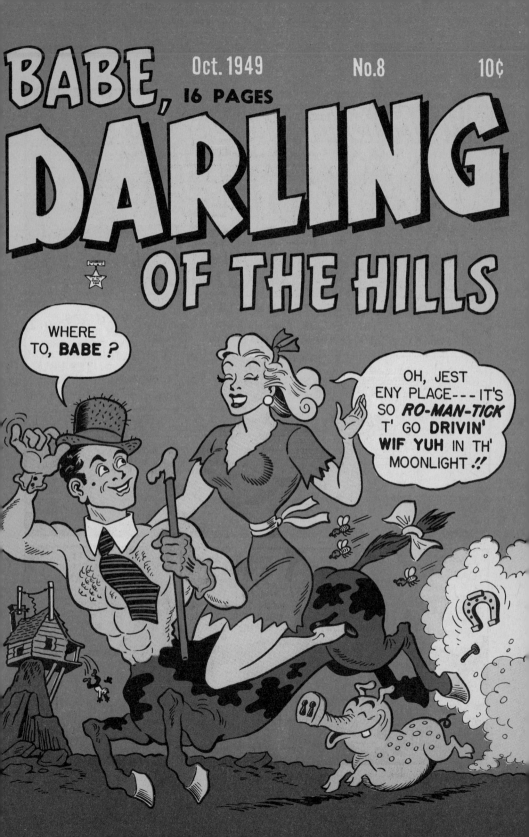

THET MAKES **SIX BEAUTIFUL GIRLS THIS MONTH** WHO HAS MYSTERIOUSLY DIS-A-PEERED UP TH' TUNNEL THET GOES T' TH' **TOP O' MYSTERY MOUNTAIN**!!

YES, AN' LAST MONTH **FORTY-ONE** BEAUTIFUL GIRLS DIS-A-PEERED UP TH' TUNNEL!

AN' MONTH BEFO' LAST THAR WUZ **SIXTY-SEVEN** BEAUTIFUL GIRLS THET WENT UP TH' TUNNEL **NEVAH** T' BE **SEEN AGAIN**!

AN' LAST YEAR **NINE HUNDRED AN' TWENTY BEAUTIFUL GIRLS** WENT UP TH' TUNNEL!

YEAR BEFO' LAST **TWO THOUSAN' AN' THIRTEEN** DIS-A-PEERED ----AN TH' YEAR BEFO' THET **EIGHT THOUSAN'** AN'---

EF SUMBODY DON'T **SOLVE TH' MYSTERY** O' MYSTERY MOUNTAIN PURTY SOON WE IS GONNA RUN **SMACK-DAB OUT** O' **BEAUTIFUL GIRLS**!!

THEN **AH VOLUNTEER** FER THIS **DANGEROUS MISSION**--- AH WILL GO **SPY** ON MYSTERY MOUNTAIN AN' **SOLVE TH' MYSTERY**!!

AH'VE HEARD THET WHEN A GIRL GETS WIF-IN **WHISTLIN' DISTANCE** O' MYSTERY MOUNTAIN SHE ACTS LIKE SHE WUZ **HIP-NO-TISED** AN' WALKS STRAIGHT T' TH' TUNNEL!

AH'LL BE CAREFUL, MAMMY-- SO WISH ME **LUCK**! AH'M OFF T' SOLVE TH' **MYSTERIOUS MYSTERY** O' **MYSTERY MOUNTAIN**!!

AH HAVE A FEELIN' IN MY BONES THET WE WILL **NEVAH** SEE OUR LI'L BABE **AGAIN**!!

AINT IT TH' **TRUFE**!

2

5

6

---IF YOU DON'T I'LL SELL YOU TO TOM---HE HAD TO **SHOOT** ONE OF HIS WHEEL PAIR LAST WEEK WHEN SHE **BROKE A LEG!**

GIDDY-YUP, BESS---PULL, JANE---GET TH' LEAD OUT, JOYCE, OR I'LL SNAP ONE ACROSS YOUR **WITHERS!!**

TOM'S DELIVERY SERVICE

IF YOU MAKE A GOOD RACER YOU'LL HAVE AN **EASY LIFE**---AND WHEN YOU'RE **TOO OLD** TO RACE YOU'LL BE **TURNED OUT TO PASTURE**---BUT IF YOU'RE A LOWLY WORK BEAST YOU'LL FINALLY END UP IN THE **GLUE FACTORY!!**

GOO FAKEY??

YES---THERE GOES AN OLD GIRL NOW! SHE'S **OUTLIVED** HER USEFULLNESS AS A PLOW PULLER---SO SHE'LL BE **RENDERED INTO GLUE** AND SPREAD ON **FLY PAPER!**

FY PAPR?

SURE! WE USE THE **GLUE** TO MAKE **HORSE-FLY PAPER!** US CENTAURS CAN'T STAND THOSE PESKY HORSE-FLIES!! SO IF **YOU** DON'T WANT TO END UP **CATCHING FLIES** YOU'D BETTER **CALM DOWN!!**

STOP TROTTIN'!

AH! THAT'S BETTER! SAY---YOU'RE A **FAST RUNNER**---YOU'LL EASILY WIN THE **DERBY** BY TEN LENGTHS!!

7

9

THE SUN GOES DOWN---THE MOON COMES UP--THE MOON GOES DOWN---THE SUN COMES UP------BY NED, 'TIS MORNING!

WAKE UP, YOU **LUCKY** GIRLS---IT'S BREAKFAST TIME---HERE'S SOME NICE, FRESH, CRISP **HAY!**

AH CAINT **SWALLER** THIS **DRY STUFF** WIFOUT SUM **MILK!** AH'VE GOTTA ESCAPE FRUM THIS MOUNTAIN BEFO AH **STARVE T' DEATH!**

YOU CAN'T ESCAPE, DEARIE-- THE TUNNEL IS THE **ONLY** EXIT--AND IT'S ALWAYS GUARDED BY **SHAGTAIL ROAN**---THE **ROUGHEST, TOUGHEST** CENTAUR OF THEM **ALL**

THERE SHE IS, BOSS---ALL BRIDLED AND REARING TO GO! **GOOD LUCK** IN THE RACE TODAY!!

THANKS, SHETLAND-- KEEP YOUR **HOOFS** CROSSED FOR ME!

BUFF GUG--BLUB FLIT BLIPS!!

WHAT DID YOU SAY, GIRL ? I CAN'T UNDERSTAND YOU WITH THAT **BIT** IN YOUR MOUTH!

AH SAID AH IS NICE AN' **GENTLE** ----SO PLEASE LEAVE TH' BRIDLE OFF---IT **SPLITS** MY **LIPS!**

DON'T BE A **SILLY FILLY!** HOW WOULD YOU KNOW WHICH WAY TO TURN IF I DIDN'T **JERK** YOUR HEAD IN THE RIGHT DIRECTION!?

YUH CUD **TELL ME**----AH UNDAHSTAN' **ANGLISH!**

OKAY---**STRIKE A TROT**----AND GO STRAIGHT AHEAD!

YES, MASTER!

10

WHOA, GIRL----WHOA! WHOA! WHOA!!

WHUT'S WRONG WIF HIM?

THAT'S MANGY MARVIN! HE'S HAD THAT GIRL THREE YEARS AND SHE RUNS AWAY WITH HIM AT LEAST TWICE EVERY DAY--- HE JUST CAN'T SEEM TO SADDLE-BREAK HER!!

WELL, HERE WE ARE AT THE RACE TRACK! I HOPE YOU CAN JUMP AS WELL AS YOU CAN RUN!

AH CAN RUN FASTER, JUMP FUTHER, DIVE DEEPER AN' CUM UP DRIER THAN ENY GIRL ON THIS FLAT-TOPPED MOUNTAIN

IF PINTO'S NEW FILLY CAN WIN TH' GRAND PRIZE HE'LL BE TH' RICHEST GUY IN CENTAUR LAND!

IT'S POST TIME--- LET'S GET DOWN TO THE RAIL AND SEE THE RACE!

NE
FAY
JOY 10-2
JUDY- 2-5
MAE 532-1

2 BALES OF HAY WINDOW

5 B
OF
TIPS

THREE OUT OF SIX MONDAY

JUST KEEP YOUR HEAD UP AND YOUR FEET UNDER YOU ON THE JUMPS!

AH'LL DO MY BEST---BUT AH'M A LI'L NERVOUS! THIS IS TH' FUST TIME AH'VE EVAH BEEN IN A HOSS RACE WIF ME CARRYIN' TH' HOSS!

WHOA, GIRL---- STEADY--

READY! GET SET!

11

THEY'RE OFF!!

HERE THEY COME-- AND PETE PINTO'S GIRL **FELL DOWN---** ---NOW SHE'S **UP---** SHE'S **DOWN** AGAIN ---SHE'S **UP---** **DOWN---UP--**

OH, MURDER !! AND I WAGERED ALL MY **OATS** ON HER !! IF I HAD ANY **HORSE-SENSE** I WOULDN'T BET ON **PEOPLE---**YOU JUST CAN'T **FIGURE** 'EM !!

GIDDY-YUP! GIDDY-YUP!!

AH'M SORRY AH GOT OFF T' SECH A PORE START---BUT AH **THREW A SHOE** !!

DON'T WORRY ABOUT IT! WE'RE IN A POCKET NOW---BUT IT'LL OPEN UP WHEN WE HIT THE **FIRST** JUMP! THE PIT IS FILLED WITH **QUICKSAND** AND THE SHORT JUMPERS ARE ELIMINATED IMMEDIATELY!

YUH MEAN BY TH' **TIME** THEY GIT OUT O' TH' QUICKSAND THEY'RE SO **FAR BEHIND** THEY DON'T HAVE A CHANCE AT WINNIN'?

THEY DON'T HAVE A CHANCE PERIOD!

SEE WHAT I MEAN?

GLUB

12

13

14

BOODY ROGERS (b.1904) IS THE OLDEST LIVING CONTRIBUTOR TO THE FIRST COMIC BOOK, THE FUNNIES. DURING HIS CAREER, HE ASSISTED ZACK MOSLEY ON SMILIN' JACK AND CREATED SPARKY WATTS. HE RETIRED FROM COMICS IN 1952 AND OPENED 2 ART SUPPLY SHOPS IN ARIZONA.

Boody's self-published autobiography, *Homeless Bound*, is available from him for $7.95 (plus $1.75 p.& h.) at 205 4th St. S.E., Childress, Texas 79201.

FROM·MARACAIBO

ITALY, ON THE SPEZIA- PARMA LINE, FRIDAY.

I'M GOING TO MELT IN THIS HEAT. WHY DON'T YOU WEAR A COAT, LIKE EVERYONE ELSE?

I DON'T HAVE A COAT.

AND WHY THE HELL DID YOU COME HERE IN THE MIDDLE OF THIS SNOW WITHOUT A COAT?

CLICK

CLACK

I CAME FOR THE DEATH OF MY MOTHER.

SORRY. THERE WAS NO WAY I COULD KNOW.

NO. ARE YOU FROM ABROAD? AN IMMIGRANT PERHAPS? BEEN HERE LONG? EXCUSE ALL THESE QUESTIONS BUT WITH THAT SHIRT...

ANSWER: A: FROM MARACAIBO. B: YES. C: A LIFETIME.

SO, THAT'S WHY THE HELL HE'S COME!

Translation by Eduardo Kaplan. Lettering by R. Sikoryak. © 1990 Altan/Quipos

MAUS

...AND HERE MY TROUBLES BEGAN...

CHAPTER NINE

Women's barracks. *Oswiecim, Poland.*   Bungalow colony. *South Fallsburg, N.Y.*

S Y N O P S I S

ART

FRANÇOISE

VLADEK

MALA

Art **Spiegelman**, a cartoonist, is working on a book about his parents' lives as Polish Jews during World War II. He is married to **Françoise**, a French woman who converted to Judaism to please his father, **Vladek**. Vladek's two heart attacks and other ailments have left him in poor health.

Art's mother, Anja, committed suicide in 1968. Vladek has been living in Rego Park, New York with his second wife, **Mala**, who is also a survivor of Hitler's Europe.

Art and his father don't get along well, and when he learns that Vladek burned Anja's memoirs after her death, he stalks off, furious.

During a vacation in Vermont, Art and Francoise get a panicked call from Vladek in his Catskills bungalow. He tells them that Mala has left him. They reluctantly agree to spend some time with him.

While they are together, he continues his story of life in Poland. In the beginning of March, 1944, after spending several years in ghettoes and months in hiding, he and Anja were caught and sent to Auschwitz, where they were separated. Working as an English tutor to a kapo, as a tinsmith, and as a shoemaker, he survived for almost a year in the camp...

MAUS, A Survivor's Tale.
Part One: "My Father Bleeds History."
ISBN 0-394-74723-2

"An epic story told in tiny pictures...a remarkable feat of documentary detail and novelistic vividness...an unfolding literary event."

—New York Times Book Review

The first six chapters, as they appeared in the pages of RAW, are available in book form at bookstores, or by mail (see "Raw Product," page 4, for ordering information).

MAUS. Chapter Nine: "And Here My Troubles Began." © 1990 art spiegelman.

And so...

LOOK, I'M SORRY I SNAPPED AT YOU BEFORE...

YES. THE WALLS ARE SO THIN, THE NEIGHBORS CAN HEAR EVERYTHING

I MEAN, FRANÇOISE AND I ARE BOTH WORRIED ABOUT YOU NOW THAT MALA IS GONE, BUT YOU CAN'T EXPECT US TO MOVE IN WITH YOU PERMANENTLY...

WHAT PERMANENTLY? I WANT ONLY YOU'LL ENJOY HERE THE SUMMER WITH ME... IT'S PAID ALREADY IN FULL, WITH NO REFUND.

HOW WILL YOU MANAGE, LIVING IN REGO PARK ALL ALONE?

ALONE I CAN MANAGE MORE EASY THAN WITH MALA, BELIEVE ME.

COME. WE'LL SIT ALL THREE TOGETHER IN THE FRONT.

Y'KNOW... LAST NIGHT I WAS READING ABOUT AUSCHWITZ...

SOME PRISONERS WORKING IN THE GAS CHAMBERS REVOLTED. THEY KILLED 3 S.S. MEN AND BLEW UP A CREMATORIUM.

YAH. FOR THIS THEY ALL GOT KILLED.

AND THE FOUR YOUNG GIRLS WHAT SNEAKED OVER THE AMMUNITIONS FOR THIS, THEY HANGED THEM NEAR TO MY WORKSHOP.

THEY WERE GOOD FRIENDS OF ANJA, FROM SOSNOWIEC. THEY HANGED A LONG, LONG TIME. SIGH.

A COUPLE WEEKS MORE AND THEY *WOULDN'T* HANG...
IT WAS VERY NEAR TO THE END, THERE IN AUSCHWITZ.

BOOM

YOU HEAR THAT, VLADEK? THE FRONT IS NO MORE THAN 25 MILES AWAY...

IF WE CAN JUST STAY ALIVE A LITTLE BIT LONGER, THE RUSSIANS WILL BE HERE.

THIS BOY WORKED IN THE OFFICE AND KNEW RUMORS.

THE GERMANS ARE GETTING WORRIED. THE BIG SHOTS HERE ARE ALREADY RUNNING BACK INTO THE REICH.

THEY'RE PLANNING TO TAKE EVERYBODY HERE BACK TO CAMPS INSIDE GERMANY. EVERYBODY!

BUT A FEW OF US HAVE A PLAN... WE'RE NOT GOING!

YOU HAVE A FRIEND IN THE CAMP LAUNDRY. HELP US GET CIVILIAN CLOTHES AND JOIN US.

HE TOOK ME QUICK TO AN ATTIC IN ONE OF THE BLOCKS.

THIS ROOM ISN'T BEING USED ANYMORE. WHEN THE EVACUATION STARTS, THE SEVEN OF US WILL COME UP HERE TO HIDE.

WE ARRANGED THERE CLOTHING AND EVEN IDENTITY PAPERS, AND HALF EACH DAY'S BREAD WE PUT OVER HERE.

WE DIDN'T STAND ON THE LAST APPELS, BUT CAME UP TO THIS ATTIC.

SCREAMING GESTAPO CHASED EVERYWHERE. EACH PRISONER GOT A BREAD, A SAUSAGE AND A KICK OUT, OUT THE GATE, TO MARCH.

THEN THIS GUY FROM THE OFFICE RAN IN....

TERRIBLE NEWS! WE HAVE TO LEAVE!

THEY'RE GOING TO SET FIRE TO THE CAMP AND BOMB ALL THE BLOCKS! HURRY!

FINALLY THEY *DIDN'T* BOMB, BUT THIS WE COULDN'T KNOW. WE LEFT BEHIND EVERY-THING, WE WERE SO AFRAID, EVEN THE CIVILIAN CLOTHES WE ORGANIZED. AND RAN OUT!

IT WAS ALREADY NIGHT, THEY GAVE TO EACH OF US A BLANKET AND A LITTLE BIT FOOD TO CARRY, AND WE WENT OUT FROM AUSCHWITZ, MAYBE THE LAST ONE.

ALL NIGHT I HEARD SHOOTING. HE WHO GOT TIRED, WHO CAN'T WALK SO FAST, THEY SHOT.

THE MORE WE WALKED, THE MORE I HEARD SHOOTING...

AND IN THE DAYLIGHT, FAR AHEAD, I SAW IT.

KRAK

SOMEBODY IS JUMPING, TURNING, ROLLING 25 OR 35 TIMES AROUND. AND STOPS.

"OH," I SAID. "THEY MAYBE KILLED THERE A DOG."

WHEN I WAS A BOY OUR NEIGHBOR HAD A DOG WHAT GOT MAD AND WAS BITING.

KPOW

THE NEIGHBOR CAME OUT WITH A RIFLE AND SHOT.

THE DOG WAS ROLLING SO, AROUND AND AROUND, KICKING, BEFORE HE LAY QUIET.

AND NOW I THOUGHT: "HOW AMAZING IT IS THAT A HUMAN BEING REACTS THE SAME LIKE THIS NEIGHBOR'S DOG."

ONE OF THE BOYS WHAT WE WERE IN THE ATTIC TOGETHER, TALKED OVER TO THE GUARD...

PSST... LOOK. THE WAR IS ALMOST OVER. SOME OF US WANT TO ESCAPE INTO THE WOODS. WE CAN PAY...

?

SHARE THIS GOLD WITH THE GUARDS IN FRONT AND BEHIND. JUST DON'T SHOOT WHEN WE RUN...

WE'LL GIVE YOU THE SIGNAL LATE TO-NIGHT, AND SHOOT OVER YOUR HEADS.

ALL DAY LONG THEY WERE ARRANGING...

IT'S ALL SET, VLADEK. HELP PAY OFF THE GUARDS AND JOIN US.

ACH. HOW CAN YOU TRUST THE GERMANS?!

AT NIGHT WAS A COMMOTION. 8 OR 9 RAN OFF...

BANG

AND OF COURSE YOU *COULDN'T* TRUST...

SO THE MARCH WAS GOING AND GOING. FOREVER WE MARCHED. AND THE ONES WHAT DIDN'T FALL DOWN, WE MARCHED.

AND SO WE CAME OVER TO GROSS-ROSEN.

HERE WAS A SMALL CAMP, WITH NO GAS.

IT WAS THOUSANDS OF PRISONERS FROM ALL AROUND BEING PULLED BACK INTO GERMANY.

EVERYWHERE WAS CONFUSION AND HITTING. TERRIBLE!

YOU SHITS OVER THERE! GO HAUL THE SOUP FROM THE KITCHEN—TWO TO EACH PAIL.

THEY CAUGHT 20 OF US TO CARRY.

YOU SEE WHAT'S GOING ON HERE. STAY WITH ME!

I GRABBED FAST A GUY WHAT WAS STILL STRONG LIKE ME.

MOST COULDN'T EVEN LIFT THEY WERE WEAK FROM MARCHING AND NO FOOD.

QUICK! QUICK!

BEHIND I HEARD YELLING AND SHOUTING. I DIDN'T LOOK.

LAZY BASTARDS! LOOK AT HOW THOSE TWO RUN!

WE GOT AN EXTRA PORTION SOUP FOR THIS. MOST WERE NOT LUCKY TO BE STILL STRONG.

IN THE MORNING THEY CHASED US TO MARCH AGAIN OUT, WHO KNOWS WHERE...

THROUGH THE TOWN WE WERE GOING. IT WAS EMPTY, WITH NO PRIVATE PEOPLE. AND WE SAW, FROM FAR, A TRAIN.

IT WAS SUCH A TRAIN FOR HORSES, FOR COWS.

INSIDE! MOVE! MOVE!

THEY PUSHED UNTIL IT WAS NO ROOM LEFT.

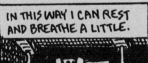

WE LAY ONE ON TOP THE OTHER, LIKE MATCHES, LIKE HERRINGS.

I PUSHED TO A CORNER NOT TO GET CRUSHED...

I HAD STILL THE THIN BLANKET THEY GAVE ME.

IN THIS WAY I CAN REST AND BREATHE A LITTLE.

HIGH UP I SAW A FEW HOOKS TO CHAIN UP MAYBE THE ANIMALS.

I CLIMBED TO SOMEBODY'S SHOULDER AND HOOKED IT STRONG.

THIS SAVED ME. MAYBE 25 PEOPLE CAME OUT FROM THIS CAR OF 200.

SO, THE TRAIN WAS GOING, WE DIDN'T KNOW WHERE.

FOR DAYS AND NIGHTS, NOTHING.

AND THEN IT **STOPPED.**

NO FOOD AND NO WATER, ONLY SCREAMS INSIDE.

YOU SEE, PEOPLE BEGAN TO DIE, TO FAINT...

AI! MY LEGS! I'M BEING STABBED!

AII!

IT WASN'T **ROOM** TO FALL ...AND IF HE FELL, THEY STOOD ON HIM.

SO HE JABBED TO THEIR LEGS WITH A KNIFE, BUT USUALLY HE ANYWAY DIED.

IF SOMEONE HAD TO MAKE A URINE OR A BOWEL MOVEMENT, HE DID WHERE HE STOOD.

IF HE HAD STILL FOOD, HE ATE IT.

I ATE MOSTLY SNOW FROM UP ON THE ROOF.

SOME HAD SUGAR SOMEHOW, BUT IT BURNED.

MY THROAT! I NEED WATER! WATER! GIVE ME SOME SNOW!

I CAN ONLY REACH A LITTLE FOR MYSELF!

PLEASE! PLEASE!! I BEG YOU!

OKAY. GIVE ME SOME SUGAR, I'LL GET YOU SOME SNOW...

SO I ATE ALSO SUGAR AND SAVED THEIR LIFE.

THE TRAIN STAYED SO, WITHOUT MOVING, I DON'T KNOW HOW LONG, UP TO A WEEK...

THEN, ONE DAY THEY OPENED...

THROW OUT THE DEAD, AND CLEAN UP YOUR FILTH!

IF THE DEAD HAD BREAD LEFT, OR BETTER SHOES, WE KEPT...

OUTSIDE WERE MANY TRAINS STANDING FOR WEEKS, WHAT THEY NEVER OPENED, AND IT WAS EVERYONE DEAD INSIDE...

...THEY DIDN'T NEED ANYMORE.

THEY CLOSED US AGAIN. WE WERE VERY HAPPY WE HAD NOW ROOM WHERE TO STAND.

NEAR TO THE DOOR WE PILED NEW DEAD ONES. EACH DAY THE GERMANS OPENED: "HOW MANY DEAD?" AND WE THREW OUT, AND SOON WE HAD ROOM EVEN TO SIT.

THEN THE TRAIN STARTED AGAIN GOING AND GOING...
INSIDE WE WERE MORE DYING AND SOME GOT CRAZY.

THEY OPENED THAT WE WILL
THROW OUT THE DEAD...

WE'VE GOTTA GET OUT!
LET US OUT! OUT! OUT!

THEN AGAIN IT STOPPED.

ALL OF
YOU-GET
DOWN!

WE COULD NOT
BELIEVE WHAT
WE ARE SEEING!

THERE IS THE
RED CROSS!...

YES! AND THE GIRLS ARE GIVING TO EVERYBODY A
SNACK - A LITTLE COFFEE AND A PIECE OF BREAD...

WE DIDN'T REMEMBER EVEN HOW
BREAD LOOKS. WE WERE VERY HAPPY.

THEN THEY CHASED US BACK IN THE TRAIN AGAIN
TO DIE, AND SO THE TRAVEL CONTINUED MORE...

FROM ALL THE CAMPS
OF EUROPE THEY NOW
BROUGHT BACK ALL OF
US INSIDE GERMANY.

IN THE MIDDLE WE FOUND OUT
THAT WE ARE COMING TO DACHAU.

THIS WAS EARLY FEBRUARY, IN 1945. IT WAS NO FOOD AND SO CROWDED —

LOOK WHERE YOU GO!

ACH! THE SHOP-RITE IS *THERE*, AND YOU DIDN'T TURN TO IT!

≈WHOOSH≈

SO, COME. WE'LL GO NOW IN TO GIVE BACK OUR GROCERIES.

NO WAY! I'M NOT GOING IN TO RETURN A LOAD OF OPEN BOXES AND PARTIALLY EATEN FOOD.

WHAT'S TO BE SO ASHAMED? IT'S FOODS I CAN'T EAT. YOU WAIT THEN IN THE CAR WHILE *I* ARRANGE IT.

Y'KNOW... I'LL BET YOU THAT ANJA'S NOTEBOOKS WERE WRITTEN ON BOTH SIDES OF THE PAGE...

HUH? I CAN'T REMEMBER. WHY D'YOU SAY THAT?

WELL... IF THERE WERE ANY *BLANK* PAGES VLADEK WOULD NEVER HAVE BURNED THEM.

UH HUH... HEY! YOU CAN SEE HIM IN THE WINDOW!

JEEZ. VLADEK AND THE MANAGER ARE SHOUTING AT EACH OTHER...

NOW THE MANAGER IS JUST WALKING AWAY FROM HIM...

AND NOW VLADEK IS TRAILING AFTER HIM...

HOW EMBARRASSING.

SIGH. I'D RATHER KILL MYSELF THAN LIVE THROUGH ALL THAT...

WHAT? RETURNING GROCERIES?

NO. EVERYTHING VLADEK WENT THROUGH. IT'S A MIRACLE HE SURVIVED.

UH-HUH. BUT IN SOME WAYS HE DIDN'T SURVIVE.

MAYBE WE SHOULD STAY WITH HIM A FEW DAYS LONGER. HE NEEDS HELP.

ARE YOU KIDDING?

...I DON'T THINK WE'D SURVIVE.

YOO-HOO!

YOU SEE? I EXCHANGED AND GOT SIX DOLLARS WORTH OF NEW GROCERIES FOR ONLY ONE DOLLAR!

INCRED-IBLE!...

...WE WERE SURE YOU'D GET KICKED OUT OF THE STORE!

WHAT ARE YOU TALKING? THE MANAGER IS A VERY FINE GENTLEMAN...

HE HELPED ME AS SOON I EXPLAINED TO HIM MY HEALTH, HOW MALA LEFT ME, AND HOW IT WAS IN THE CAMPS.

OY! GET IN... WE CAN'T EVER SHOW OUR FACES HERE AGAIN.

NOW WE'LL DRIVE BACK SO I CAN PHONE TO MY LAWYER ON MALA.

DACHAU... YOU WERE SAYING IT WAS VERY CROWDED IN THAT CAMP...

YAH—THIS WAS A CAMP—TERRIBLE! I HAD A MISERY, I CAN'T TELL YOU,... HERE, IN DACHAU, MY TROUBLES BEGAN.

WE WERE CLOSED IN BARRACKS, SITTING ON STRAW, WAITING ONLY TO DIE.

IN THE STRAW, IT WAS LICE...

FROM THE LICE WAS TYPHUS.

TO EAT WE GOT ONLY BREAD AND SOUP, BUT YOU HAD TO SHOW FIRST YOUR SHIRT...

IF IT WAS ANY LICE, YOU GOT NO SOUP. THIS WAS IMPOSSIBLE. EVERYWHERE WAS LICE!

AND, GOD FORBID, IF SOMEONE GOT SOUP AND SOMEONE SPILLED HIM A DROP...

LIKE WILD ANIMALS THEY WOULD FIGHT UNTIL THERE WAS BLOOD.

YOU CAN'T KNOW WHAT IT IS, TO BE HUNGRY.

THERE, IN DACHAU, I GOT AN INFECTION IN MY HAND...

I TRIED TO MAKE WORSE AND WORSE MY INFECTION...

I WANTED THEY TAKE ME TO THE INFIRMARY.

EACH FEW DAYS SOMEONE CAME TO SEE WHO IS SICK...

GO WITH THEM...

YOU SEE, THE INFIRMARY, I HEARD IT WAS A PARADISE.

PUT THIS OINTMENT ON HIS HAND AND KEEP IT BANDAGED. IT WILL CLEAR UP QUICKLY.

HERE I HAD THREE TIMES A DAY SOMETHING TO EAT, AND IT WAS ONLY TWO PATIENTS FOR EACH BED.

I WORKED HOW I COULD WITH ONE HAND, SO THEY WILL LIKE ME.

THAT'S STRANGE, IT SHOULD HAVE HEALED BY NOW!

I IRRITATED EACH DAY MY HAND, TO STAY LONGER.

AII!

THERE! I OPENED IT UP AGAIN!

THIS HURT ME REALLY VERY VERY MUCH...

I GOT AFRAID FOR MY HAND AND LET IT HEAL.

...I HAVE STILL TODAY A SCAR ON THIS PLACE.

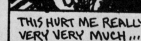

FROM THE INFIRMARY I HAD TO GO BACK TO A BAD BARRACK, WHERE WE WERE ALL DAY STANDING OUTSIDE.

PARLEZ-VOUS FRANÇAIS?

WHA? NO...

IT WAS NOTHING TO EAT, AND NOTHING TO DO, ONLY TO WAIT AND TO DIE.

I CAN SPEAK GERMAN, YIDDISH, POLISH AND ENGLISH.

ANGLAIS?!

DIEU MERCI! I TALK ENGLISH ALSO A LITTLE. I WAS BECOMING CRAZY!...

THERE IS NO OTHER FRENCH HERE AND I DO NOT KNOW TO TALK GERMAN. I HAD NOBODY TO WHO TO TALK.

YOU ARE A POLE-JEW, YES? HOW YOU KNOW ENGLISH?

ACCH... I DREAMED ALWAYS TO GO ONE DAY TO AMERICA...

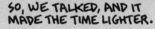

SO, WE TALKED, AND IT MADE THE TIME LIGHTER.

EACH DAY HE FOUND ME, THE FRENCH MAN...

BRR. GOOD MORNING. IT IS AGAIN VERY COLD TODAY.

LOOK TO THIS, MY FRIEND. I HAVE A BOX!

HE WAS NOT A JEW, SO BY THE RED CROSS THEY LET PACKAGES COME TO HIM.

MY FAMILY SENDS. I WANT THAT YOU ALSO EAT SOMETHING.

MY GOD. SARDINES! BISCUITS! CHOCOLATE!

HE INSISTED TO SHARE WITH ME, AND IT SAVED ME MY LIFE.

WITH MY NEW FOOD I CAME TO AN IDEA...

PSST- DO YOU WANT TO BUY A BAR OF CHOCOLATE?

CHOCOLATE?! DO I LOOK LIKE A MILLIONAIRE?

I'LL TRADE IT FOR YOUR SHIRT.

MY SHIRT?! YOU'RE CRAZY- I'D FREEZE!

UM- GIVE ME YOUR DAY'S RATION OF BREAD TOO.

IN AUSCHWITZ A SHIRT WAS NOT SO EX- PENSIVE, BUT HERE NO GOODS CAME IN.

I CLEANED THE SHIRT VERY, VERY CAREFUL.

AND OUTSIDE, I DRIED IT.

I WAS LUCKY TO FIND A PIECE OF PAPER...

SO, CAREFUL I WRAPPED IT.

I UNWRAPPED ONLY WHEN THEY CALLED TO SOUP...

HERE WAS A SHIRT WITH REALLY NO LICE!

MY OLD SHIRT I HID TO MY PANTS. I SHOWED THE NEW ONE.

OKAY.

RIGHT AWAY THEY GAVE ME TO EAT.

YOU ARE A GENIUS, VLADEK. A GENIUS!

I HELPED THE FRENCHMAN TO ALSO ORGANIZE A SHIRT, SO WE BOTH GOT ALWAYS SOUP.

BUT AFTER A FEW WEEKS I GOT TOO SICK EVEN TO EAT...

TYPHUS!

I GOT VERY HOT FEVER AND I COULDN'T SLEEP. *TYPHUS!*

EVERY NIGHT PEOPLE DIED OF THIS.

AT NIGHT I HAD TO GO TO THE TOILET DOWN. IT WAS ALWAYS FULL, THE WHOLE CORRIDOR, WITH THE DEAD PEOPLE PILED THERE. YOU COULDN'T GO THROUGH...

YOU HAD TO GO ON THEIR HEADS, AND THIS WAS TERRIBLE, BECAUSE IT WAS SO SLIPPERY, THE SKIN, YOU THOUGHT YOU ARE FALLING. AND THIS WAS EVERY NIGHT.

SO NOW I HAD TYPHUS, AND I HAD TO GO TO THE TOILET DOWN, AND I SAID, "NOW IT'S MY TIME. NOW I WILL BE LAYING LIKE THIS ONES AND SOMEBODY WILL STEP ON ME!"

I WAS ALIVE STILL THE NEXT TIME IT CAME A GUY FROM THE INFIRMARY...

MANY DIDN'T LIVE LONG ENOUGH TO GO TO DIE IN THE INFIRMARY.

THERE I LAY TOO WEAK EVEN TO MOVE OR TO GO TO THE TOILET OUT FROM BED.

I ASKED HELP FROM THE FELLOWS NEXT TO ME, BUT IN A FEW HOURS THEY WERE DEAD AND OTHERS CAME.

THEY GAVE BREAD AND SOUP, BUT I WAS TOO WEAK TO EAT...

SO I PUT MY PORTION BELOW MY PILLOW.

HEY! THERE'S STALE BREAD ALL OVER THIS ONE'S BED!

WELL, TAKE IT AWAY... HE'LL NEVER NEED IT.

I SCREAMED. BUT I **COULDN'T** SCREAM.

MMUH MMNH.

I WAS TOO WEAK TO SCREAM...

SO I TOOK MY SHOE AND KNOCKED LOUD.

KLAKK KLAKK KLAKK

STOP THAT RACKET!

BAH! KEEP YOUR DAMN BREAD!

I COULDN'T EAT, BUT I CUT PIECES TO PAY FOR HELP TO GO DOWN TO THE TOILET.

SO... MY FEVER FELL DOWN, AND SOMETHING NEW CAME.

ATTENTION!...

EVERYONE STRONG ENOUGH TO TRAVEL, LINE UP OUTSIDE...

YOU WILL BE EXCHANGED AS WAR PRISONERS AT THE SWISS BORDER.

WAS I DREAMING ONLY?!

THEY LIKED TO SEND OUT THE SICK ONES, BUT NOT **SO** SICK THAT WE ARRIVE DEAD.

I WAS VERY WEAK, BUT FOR MY BREAD I HAD TWO FRIENDS WHAT HELPED ME.

WHEN THEY LEFT ME GO FOR EVEN A SECOND, MY LEGS DIDN'T HOLD ME.

BUT I CAME SOMEHOW OUTSIDE THE GATE...

GASP! A TRAIN!

HERE WAS A TRAIN NOT FOR COWS AND HORSES, BUT A REAL TRAIN TO TAKE PASSENGERS - A TRAIN FOR **PEOPLE!**

I THOUGHT THIS TRAIN, IT MUST BE FOR THE *GESTAPO*, BUT **NO!**

IT TOOK US OUT FROM DACHAU, IN THE DIRECTION TO SWITZERLAND.

WHATEVER HAPPENED TO THAT FRENCH GUY WHO HELPED YOU?

YAH. HE WAS A FINE FELLOW...

I CAN'T REMEMBER EVEN HIS NAME, BUT IN PARIS HE IS LIVING... FOR YEARS WE EXCHANGED LETTERS IN THE ENGLISH I TAUGHT TO HIM.

WELL..DID YOU SAVE ANY OF HIS LETTERS?

OF COURSE I SAVED. BUT ALL THIS I THREW AWAY TOGETHER WITH ANJA'S NOTEBOOKS.

ALL SUCH THINGS OF THE WAR, I TRIED TO PUT OUT FROM MY MIND ONCE FOR ALL... UNTIL YOU *REBUILD* ME ALL THIS FROM YOUR QUESTIONS.

?!

HAH?! WHAT FOR DO YOU STOP, FRANÇOISE? WE'RE NOT YET TO THE BUNGALOW!

THERE'S A HITCH-HIKER...

SKREEEEEK!

A HITCH-HIKER? AND -OY- IT'S A COLORED GUY, A SHVARTSER!

HIYA.

PUSH QUICK ON THE GAS!

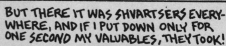

To be continued.

THE CHILD SLAVE REBELLION

When his landlord, photographer Nathan Lerner, entered Henry Darger's room in 1972, he was faced with mountains of the old man's scavengings accumulated over the 40 years he had lived there: crucifixes, broken toys and dolls, bundles of old magazines and comic books, piles of phone directories used to paste-in complete runs of *Nancy* clipped from the daily paper, 88 pairs of broken eyeglasses, hundreds of empty bottles of Pepto Bismol, 500 pairs of dilapidated shoes, balls of twine that he had made from tying small pieces together; the list was endless. Henry Darger, who spent most of his adult life as an industrious janitor scrubbing Chicago's hospitals from 7 am to 8:30 pm, came home to create a fantastic world collaged from the debris of popular culture in the privacy of his own never-cleaned room.

In 1916, at age 24, Darger began typing what turned into a 19,000 page epic: *The Adventures of the Vivian Girls in What is Known as the Realms of the Unreal or the Glandelinian War Storm or the Glandico-Abiennian Wars, as caused by the Child Slave Rebellion*. It is the story of a planet (of which our earth is a moon) where all the countries are Catholic. But one, Glandelinia, turns against the faith and enslaves, tortures, mutilates and murders its children. The beautiful Vivian Girls eventually save them with the help of the Hero, Jack Evans. Darger handbound each of the 13 volumes and inscribed the title in gold leaf. To illustrate the story, he painted 87 wall-size paintings on both sides of cheap paper, glued into two-by-eight-foot sheets. The illustrations are traced and collaged from children's books, coloring books and comics. His writing "collages" and paraphrases the books that shaped his imagination: dime novels and the Bible.

The following excerpts from his first couple of hundred pages of his autobiography, written in the last 6 years of his life when illness forced him to retire, give us virtually the only information we have about Henry, the orphan boy. The rest of his autobiography is consumed by a 1,500 page description of a twister in Countybrown, Illinois, witnessed when he was 21. Darger was obsessed with Catholicism, fires, tortured children, mythical demons... and weather. Convinced that the weather was God's domain, he was deeply upset by the idea that men would attempt to predict it. He kept a daily journal, *Weather Report of Cold and Warm, Also Summer Heats and Cool Spells, Storms and Fair or Cloudy Days, Contrary to What the Weatherman Says, And Also True Too*, noting every night for 9 years what the day's forecast had been and what had actually happened.

At the age of 80, Darger's increasing lameness forced him to ask his landlord to take him to the Little Sisters of the Poor's home. He died 6 months later. ❑

The History of my life. By Henry Joseph Darger, (Dargarius ? in Brazilian), 851 Webster ave. Chicago Ill. Box 14,

In the month of april, on the 12. in the year of 1892, of what week day I never knew, as I was never told, nor did I seek the information.

Also I do not remem- ber the day my mother died, or who adopted my baby sister, as I was then too young, nor who my uncle Charles would tell me, or did not know either,

I will have to say all my child hood days with my father who was very busy every day, except sundays and holidays were sort of unevent

time to mention here.

The knee pain at night I must confess and am not ashamed to tell of it, I actually shook my fist twards heaven.

I did not mean it for God though, though I felt like it

What sin it was if it was one I do not know for sure but when I told it in confession the priest was disturbed admonished me, and gave me a severe or long prayer penance to re-

cite: Yet the severe knee pain drove me to it.

I had to quit and the doctor who I went to and examined my leg advised me to re-tire.

I did so depending on my Social Security. I retired november 19 1963. Have been retired since and I'll say it is a lazy life and I dont like it.

I suppose a real lazy person would enjoy it.

COME WE WILL CARRY THE OTHERS FOR YOU. ITS GOING TO STORM"

I do wish I could be back working there again. To make matters worse now I'm an artist, been one for years and cannot hardly stand on my feet because of my knee to paint on the top of the long picture.

Yet off and on on I try and sit down when ache or pain starts, I remember when I and a tall man were walking down Webster ave home ward bound at dark in late fall we saw an auto driver without head lights on strike a dog, nearly killing the animal right there and then nearly being hit by a can coming from the west.

I wished who we had been motorcycle cops then. We would have arrested him.

I go to three morning masses and Communion, at the seven thirty mass every day, and one extra mass on Sunday after noon at five oclock besides the seven fifteen A m and the eight Thirty.

And on mondays I go to the miraculous medal novena devotions It too is followed by a mass.

What did you say?. I am being a saint? Ha Ha. I am one, and a very sorry Saint I am, Ha Ha, How can I be a saint when I wont stand for trials bad luck, pains in my ('korn? knees or otherwise.

Manuscript excerpts courtesy Henry Darger Foundation. THANKS to Randall Morris (Cavin Morris Gallery, New York), John Ollman (Janet Fleisher Gallery, Philadelphia), Ron Jagger (Phyllis Kind Gallery, New York), and Todd Bockley (Bockley Gallery, Minneapolis).

I FELL ASLEEP WAITING FOR HER.

THROUGHOUT THE DAY SHE FINDS ANIMALS.

AND BRINGS THEM TO MY ROOM AT NIGHT.

WHERE ARE YOU?

...DEAD OR DYING

SHE KEEPS THEM UNDER MY BED.

WELL, THAT WAS TYPICAL.

YOU COME HERE EVERY NIGHT BUT YOU NEVER STAY. I DON'T UNDERSTAND...

WHAT DO YOU WANT FROM ME? YOU SPEAK TO ME AND MY EARS POP.

NOTHING IS CLEAR!

WILL YOU SHUT UP AND LOOK AT YOUR SHOES!

YOU ASK TOO MANY QUESTIONS. JUST...

Shhh... hhh.

SHHHHHHHHHH

RIBBET

WELL, I HAVE TO GO NOW.
!
I'LL BE BACK TOMMOROW NIGHT.
OUCH!
WAIT!
WHAT THE HELL DO I DO WITH ALL THESE ANIMALS!

"Good ol' Gregor Brown" by SIKORYAK

GOOD GRIEF! WHAT'S HAPPENED TO ME?

I WENT TO BED FEELING OKAY, BUT NOW...! WHAT AN AWFUL LIFE I HAVE!!

MAYBE IF I REST HERE FOR A FEW MINUTES, EVERYTHING WILL GO BACK TO NORMAL...

GREGOR! WAKE UP! YOU'RE LATE FOR WORK!

GREGOR, THIS IS YOUR MANAGER...

I HATE TO SAY THIS IN YOUR OWN HOME, BUT I MUST TELL YOU HOW DISAPPOINTED WE ARE IN YOUR RECENT BEHAVIOR...

SIR, PLEASE LET ME EXPLAIN! AS SOON AS I OPEN THIS DOOR, I'LL SOOTHE ALL YOUR FEARS!

AAUGH!!

SIR, WHERE ARE YOU GOING?

EVERYBODY, PLEASE, CALM DOWN! I'M IN A TIGHT SPOT, BUT WE CAN WORK SOMETHING OUT!

MOM, WON'T YOU LISTEN?

GOD HELP ME!

MY STOMACH HURTS!

I'VE BEEN CRAWLING THE WALLS FOR HOURS! I'VE GOT TO RELAX!

IT'S PEACEFUL ON THE CEILING... I WONDER HOW LONG I CAN STICK UP HERE...

Z

WUMP!

GRETE IS CLEARING MY THINGS OUT OF MY ROOM!
SHE CAN'T DO THAT! I'M STILL PART OF THE FAMILY! I WON'T HIDE QUIETLY WHILE SHE TAKES AWAY EVERYTHING I LOVE!
I'LL CRAWL OUT INTO THE OPEN! SHE HAS TO RESPECT MY RIGHTS!
GREGOR, YOU BLOCKHEAD!!
I DIDN'T MEAN TO UPSET GRETE LIKE THAT!
UH-OH, HERE COMES DAD! I HOPE HE'S NOT ANGRY AT ME!
HEY, WHAT'S HE DOING WITH ALL THOSE APPLES?
BONK!
I CAN'T SLEEP...
I'VE BECOME A BURDEN ON THE FAMILY... THEY CAN'T BE BOTHERED WITH ME... NOTHING SATISFIES MY DESIRES... MY OLD WAY OF LIFE IS JUST A DISTANT MEMORY...
SIGH
THAT MUSIC! ... I... I NEVER REALIZED HOW BEAUTIFUL GRETE'S PLAYING IS... !
FINALLY, I'VE FOUND SOMETHING WORTHWHILE! I'VE GOT TO SHOW HER MY APPRECIATION! I'LL DO ANYTHING FOR HER!
GET LOST, YOU STUPID BUG!!
BRIGHT AND EARLY, THE MAID ENTERS THE BROWN HOUSEHOLD...
!
HAPPINESS IS A PEST-FREE HOME!

© 1990 R. Sikoryak

THE CORNE

The Collapsible Table Company

LOCATION

The Drink of Life

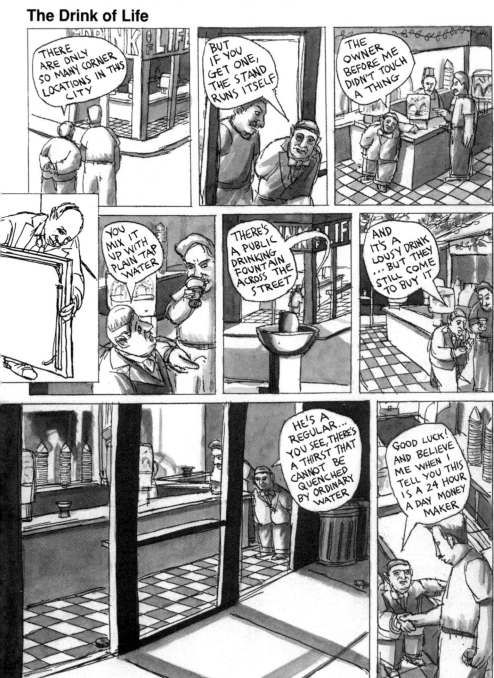

The Collapsible Table Company *(continued)*

The Drink of Life *(continued)*

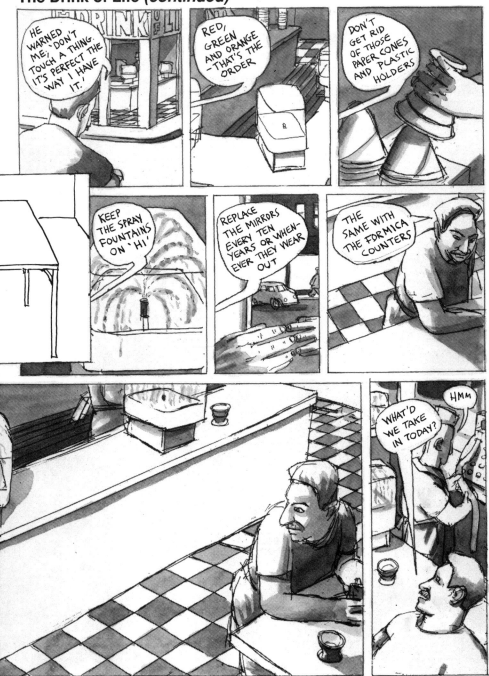

The Collapsible Table Company *(continued)*

The Drink of Life *(continued)*

I TOOK THE OLD MAN'S ADVICE AND DIDN'T TOUCH A THING

BUT THE PLACE NEEDED A PAINT JOB

AND THOSE PLASTIC VINES WERE FILTHY

AND I TOOK IN ONE NEW DRINK

IT'S NOT FOR THE CUSTOMER'S SAKE. I HAVE TO LOOK AT THE PLACE EVERYDAY

10 P.M. THAT SALESMAN — THE REGULAR — DID HE COME IN?

NO, IT WAS A SLOW DAY

I DON'T BELIEVE IT. IN THIS BUSINESS ALL YOU NEED IS A GOOD LOCATION

REALITY

Marti

IN A DARK ALLEY ON THE OUTSKIRTS OF A SPANISH TOWN, ONE MAN STABS ANOTHER....

AS A RESULT, THE VICTIM DIES...

THE KILLER SEARCHES THE POCKETS OF THE CORPSE SPRAWLED ON THE PAVEMENT, AND THEN FLEES...

THE AGGRESSOR KILLED THE MAN FOR THE 970* PESETAS HE HAD BEEN CARRYING...

*124 PTAS = $1.00

BEFORE DYING, THE VICTIM DIDN'T KNOW THAT HIS LIFE WAS WORTH ONLY 970 PESETAS...

THE AGGRESSOR HAS CUT SHORT 43 YEARS OF EXISTENCE, EMOTIONS, FAMILY TIES, WORK AND SWEAT, BELIEFS, ILLUSIONS, DISAPPOINT- MENTS AND JOYS, FOR ONLY 970 PESETAS.

Translation by Robert Legault and Eduardo Kaplan. Lettering by Jonathan Shapiro. © 1989 Marti

A FAMILY, A FRIEND, A WIFE, SOME COMRADES, A NEIGHBOR, CAN NO LONGER HAVE THE COMPANIONSHIP OF THAT BODY LYING ON THE GROUND BECAUSE OF THAT INSTRUMENT...

THIS INSTRUMENT IS SOLD IN STORES FOR 1390 PESETAS...

ASSUMING HE BOUGHT IT, THE AGGRESSOR WOULD HAVE LOST 420 PESETAS AFTER THE MURDER...

HE DID, IN FACT, BUY IT...

THE NEXT DAY, NEWS OF THE MURDER OF A MAN IN A DARK ALLEY COMES OUT IN THE PAPER...

A CARTOONIST READS THE NEWS AND GETS AN IDEA FOR A STORY...

Thirst FOR Blood

—I'LL KILL YOU!
—ARRGH!

—BLOOD!
—BLOOD ON MY HANDS ONCE AGAIN...THE HANDS OF A RUTHLESS EXECUTIONER THIRSTING FOR **THE RED FLUID OF LIFE!**

—THESE HANDS THAT WILL GO ON KILLING... GO ON TO STAIN THEMSELVES WITH THE BLOOD OF ANOTHER **INNOCENT AND HAPLESS VICTIM UNFORTUNATE** ENOUGH TO CROSS MY PATH...

—CHILDREN, OLD FOLKS, PREGNANT WOMEN... THEY ALL CAN FALL INTO THE CLUTCHES OF THIS MONSTER BORN TO KILL... BORN TO DESTROY ANYTHING THAT MOVES AND BREATHES...

BECAUSE THIS MONSTER NEEDS HIS DOSE OF DRUGS...ALWAYS... AND MONEY TO GET IT... AND THEN MORE AND MORE AND MORE...

—BLOOD...
...MONEY...
...DRUGS...

END

THE CARTOONIST WATCHES THE WIDOW AND SOME OF HER CHILDREN ON TV. THEY LOOK VERY FRIGHTENED.

TWO DAYS LATER, THE POLICE PICK UP THE KILLER, WHO IS ALMOST LYNCHED BY THE CROWD.

HE TURNS OUT TO BE A BOOK-KEEPER WHO'D BEEN ROBBED A FEW TIMES IN THAT SEEDY AREA. SCARED BY THE VICTIM, WHO SEEMED TO BE FOLLOWING HIM, HE CONFRONTED THE MAN AND, IN THE STRUGGLE STABBED HIM WITH THE KITCHEN KNIFE HE CARRIED FOR SELF DEFENSE.

PANICKING, HE SIMULATED A ROBBERY TO THROW THE POLICE OFF THE TRACK...

THREE DAYS LATER, IT'S LEARNED THAT THE DEAD MAN WAS A DRUG DEALER...

THE CARTOONIST THINKS IT OVER... BURNS THE PAGE AND DECIDES TO DEVOTE HIS TALENT TO ADVERTISING.

END

mc guire